DATE		

THE PARENTS' BOOK
ON CALCULATORS

THE PARENTS' BOOK ON CALCULATORS

What You Should Know About Calculators and Your Child's Education

KENNETH P. GOLDBERG

OXFORD UNIVERSITY PRESS
Oxford   New York   Toronto   Melbourne
1983

OXFORD UNIVERSITY PRESS
Oxford   London   Glasgow
New York   Toronto   Melbourne   Auckland
Delhi   Bombay   Calcutta   Madras   Karachi
Kuala Lumpur   Singapore   Hong Kong   Tokyo
Nairobi   Dar es Salaam   Cape Town

and associate companies in
Beirut   Berlin   Ibadan   Mexico City   Nicosia

Library of Congress Cataloging in Publication Data

Goldberg, Kenneth P.
  The parents' book on calculators.

  Includes index.
  1. Calculating-machines. I. Title.
QA75.G588 1983   510'.7'8   83-2340
ISBN 0-19-503282-9
ISBN 0-19-503283-7 (pbk.)

Printing (last digit):   9 8 7 6 5 4 3 2 1

Printed in the United States of America

To Jeanne, Timothy, and
Rebecca who inspired me, and
encouraged me, and made the
writing of this book possible.

Contents

THE PARENTS' BOOK
ON CALCULATORS

1
Why Parents Need to Know About Calculators

This book is about calculators and their effects on education, and it is written primarily for parents and others concerned with the education of children. Since I've written it, it is reasonable to infer that *I* think parents need to be knowledgeable about, and involved in, the way calculators are being used in the schools. Furthermore, since you have bought this book (or are at least taking the time and effort to glance through it), it is most likely that you agree with me and probably have some specific questions and concerns you would like addressed. Even so, it's important to begin a book of this type by seriously examining the question raised in the title of this chapter so that the reasons for writing it and reading it are more explicitly recognized and understood. Before we proceed, however, a brief history of the calculator's impact on the schools, its "acceptance" and "rejection" by the educational community, and its current status as an educational "issue" will be helpful in setting the stage for our discussion.

Hand-held electronic calculators first became widely available and reasonably inexpensive in the early 1970s as a result of technological advances connected with the U.S. space project. Their impact on our society was so pervasive, and their potential in education so obvious and so startling, that questions began to be raised almost immediately about their effect on education by both educators and laymen. For example, on August 20, 1972, the *New York Times* ran an article titled "Hand-held Calculators: Tool or Toy?" And in the December 1973 issue of *The Arithmetic Teacher* (the official publication of the National Council of Teachers of Mathematics for elementary school level mathematics) there was an article "Hand-held Calculators: Help or Hindrance?" written by Frank S. Hawthorne, at the time the Chief of the Bureau of Mathematics Education in the New York State Education Department. In this early article an important statement was made concerning the need to use the calculator as an *aid* to the learning of mathematics rather than as a replacement for the learning of mathematics.

One of the first educational organizations to officially endorse the use of calculators in the schools was the National Council of Teachers of Mathematics (NCTM). In 1974 the Board of Directors of the NCTM approved a position statement supporting the use of calculators as instructional aids and encouraging mathematics teachers to use calculators " . . . in imaginative ways to reinforce learning and to motivate learners so they become proficient in mathematics." Other educators and educational organizations were not far behind in recognizing the potential of calculators for education. In 1974 the Conference Board of the Mathematical Sciences formed a committee to examine the status of mathematics teaching in kindergarten through high school. This committee was called the National Advisory Committee on Mathematics Education (NACOME), and the report it issued in 1975 included a recommendation that a calculator be made available for *each* mathematics student during *each* mathematics class no later than by the end of the eighth grade.

The issue of calculator use was now becoming such a heated topic among educators that the following year the National Science Foundation (NSF) funded a report on the subject. This report, titled *Electronic Hand-Calculators: The Implications for Pre-College Education,* was published in 1976 and, among its other conclusions, recommended that a calculator be provided for every student for unlimited use at the senior high school level. Also in 1976, the National Institute of Education (NIE) and the NSF jointly sponsored a conference aimed at identifying the specific questions about calculator use in education toward which research should be directed. One of the specific recommendations of this conference, as published in the conference report, was that "The education community, especially mathematics educators, must accept a leadership role in helping schools adjust to the existence of calculators." Finally, in a Joint Report of the

Mathematics Association of America (MAA) and the NCTM published in 1977 and titled "Recommendations for the Preparation of High School Students for College Mathematics Courses," the recommendation was made that " . . . computers and calculators be used in imaginative ways to reinforce learning and to motivate the student as proficiency in mathematics is gained."

In spite of these endorsements there has been, from the very first, controversy over what use to make of calculators in the classroom and their possibly harmful effects on the learning of mathematics. The major concern of those who opposed calculators was that their availability would make the teaching and learning of computation unimportant; and that, as a consequence, students would learn to press calculator keys instead of learning to think and to do basic arithmetic. Most knowledgeable mathematics educators, however, have made it clear that they are aware of this danger and that they believe the calculator can be used to enhance the learning of mathematics rather than to replace this learning. In particular, advocates of calculator use in the classroom warn about the danger of thinking of calculators in the extremes of "all good" or "all bad." This point is eloquently made by Max S. Bell of the University of Chicago in the article "Calculators in Secondary School Mathematics" (*The Mathematics Teacher*, NCTM, May 1978):

> But such a good-bad dichotomy is obviously far too simplistic. The questions are not simply whether to use or not to use calculators, but how, with whom, when, in what ways, and in the service of what objectives. . . . It is pleasing to report that the mathematics teaching profession saw almost immediately the complexity and importance of the issues surrounding calculators.

The current situation regarding calculators in the schools and the reaction of the educational community to them is probably best summed up by the following statements from the publication *The Use of Calculators in Pre-College Education: Fourth Annual State-of-the-Art Review* by Marilyn N. Suydam (Calculator Information Center, Ohio State University, August 1981):

> The technological tool that has captured the attention and imagination of educators during this past year is the microcompu-

ter—but calculators are still in schools, quietly being put to use. Their continuing use is not usually a contentious issue, as it was in the mid-1970s; rather, they are an increasingly accepted tool. . . . While all children do not use calculators in schools, and while those who do use calculators may not be using them in an integrated fashion, nevertheless it would appear that whether or not calculators should be used is no longer the foremost issue on the educational scene.

Now that we have a somewhat better perspective on where the calculator came from and where it stands today in relation to education, let's return to the question of why a parent needs to know anything about this subject.

The major point to keep in mind is that while most educators now accept calculators and the fact that they will play a part in the education of our children, the difficult questions regarding just *what* part they will play have yet to be answered. After all, the calculator revolution has only been in effect for twelve or so years; and it was only in 1976 that the joint NIE and NSF "Conference on Needed Research and Development on Hand-Held Calculators in School Mathematics" took a first step in identifying the specific questions that research into the use of calculators in the schools needed to answer. An enormous amount of research into these questions has been carried out, and is still being carried out, but it will be a while before the answers to most of these questions are known and can start to be implemented. Of course, by the 1990s a great deal of this should be pretty well worked out and we should be well on our way to incorporating the calculator into the classroom in a correct and integrated fashion. But your children are not going to school in the 1990s, they are going to school in the 1980s, and the place of the calculator in education is still being investigated.

Teachers, of course, are caught in the middle of all this. On the one hand, they do not have the experience of having learned their own mathematics with the calculator to help them in adapting their teaching to this new tool, the majority of them having gone through school before, or at least in the early stages of, the calculator revolution. In addition, they have not had formal training in the use of calculators in teaching since this was not, and in most cases is still not, one of the standard topics covered in the so-called methods courses in which teachers learn many of the skills and procedures of teaching. On the other hand, with virtually all educational organizations involved in the teaching of mathematics endorsing and often demanding that calculators be made a part of the educational process, teachers are being forced to learn about this topic on an individual basis. No wonder there is a lack of consistency and agreement, sometimes even among different teachers in the same mathematics department, as to when the calculator should be used, how it should be used, or even if it should be used at all.

Teachers are attempting to learn about calculators and to cope with the demands that they use calculators and allow their students to use calculators in a variety of ways. One way is to attend national, or regional, or even local mathematics education conferences and meetings at which talks on teaching with the calculator are given. Another way is to attend short workshops, either in the schools or at nearby teacher training institutions and universities, where classroom teachers are given help by experts in incorporating the calculator into courses they are currently teaching. Teachers can also become informed about calculator use and be up to date in new developments and research findings by reading educational journals and magazines which are increasingly publishing material in this area. Finally, the topic of calculator use in the classroom is slowly but surely becoming a part of the methods courses in which new teachers are being trained.

Unfortunately, these attempts to help present and future teachers make better use of calculators in their teaching have run into obstacles. The major obstacle, as indicated earlier, is that most questions as to how and when calculators can best be employed simply have not yet been definitively answered. Because of this, the information provided at meetings and workshops and in journal articles is not always consistent and sometimes can even be contradictory. A second obstacle is that there are no general quidelines as to when to use calculators, how to use calculators, or even whether to use calculators in different states, in different school districts within the same state, or even within the math department of one school. All of these decisions are usually left up to the individual teachers and result in a great deal of inconsistency and confusion for both teachers and students. Another obstacle to the implementation of calculators in the classroom is the lack of adequate instructional materials that incorporate the calculator as a teaching and learning tool. While some publishing companies are attempting to incorporate calculator material into their new texts, this is a slow process and will take several years at a minimum. For the near future it appears that teachers who want to use calculators as a part of their teaching must either purchase supplementary calculator materials on dwindling school budgets (or even out of their own money) or develop their own supplementary materials. Most teachers do not have the time to do this and simply are not specialist enough in calculator use to be able to do this. And, to be honest, this is not and should not be their responsibility. If for no other reason, this lack of available, good calculator-oriented texts and other materials keeps many teachers who might want to make use of the calculator from either using it at all or using it to its full potential.

If all schools and all mathematics teachers were making appropriate use of calculators by introducing them at the correct grade level; teaching the students how to use them correctly and efficiently; advising students and parents as to which calculators to purchase and which special features and function keys they should have; using calculators in imaginative ways with appropriate topics and avoiding calculator use with inappropriate topics; then it would be less essential that parents know about this subject. However, this is not the case. If the parent of a school-age child wants to know if calculators are being used in his/her child's school, how they are being used and what guidelines exist for their use, and whether the teachers who are teaching with this new tool have actually had any instruction in its use or become knowledgeable about it in some other way, then the parent simply must become an informed consumer of the education that the child is receiving. The parent can then have input into how the school is responding to this new technological tool and make sure that it is not being either misused or not used at all. If one thing has become clear from the research done on calculator use up to this time, it is the following: when calculators are used in the classroom in appropriate and imaginative ways, and by a competent and knowledgeable teacher, their use virtually never results in lower achievement than if calculators were not used; their use often results in higher achievement than if calculators were not used; and their use almost always results in higher motivation and interest in learning than if calculators were not used. Knowing this, it would be extremely unfortunate for a parent who cares about his/her child's education not to become as fully informed as possible about this subject so that he/she can have a say in making sure the calculator is put to its most beneficial use.

In Chapter 2 we will look at how the calculator is actually being used in different schools and at different grade levels. With this information as a base, you will then be able to compare the uses your child's school *is* making of the calculator with the uses it *could be* making of this machine. And, if it is not being used to its full potential, or if the teachers in the school have not received the kind of instruction, information, and materials that are needed to make the best use of it, you will be in a position to determine this and have input into correcting the situation. In most cases you do not have the option of taking your child out of a school that is not taking advantage of the existence of calculators as well as they might and placing him/her in one that is. But if you are an aware and informed consumer of the education your child is receiving, you do have the option of making your voice heard if you think the calculator is not being put to its most educationally beneficial use and insisting that in the future it is. The purpose of this book is to help you become such an aware and informed consumer.

2

How Calculators Are Being Used in Today's Schools

In Chapter 1 we touched briefly on one of the major concerns of both parents and educators regarding the "intrusion" of calculators into the classroom, in particular into the elementary school classroom. This was the concern that students would begin to use calculators for numerical computation instead of learning basic number facts or how to do simple arithmetic computations with paper and pencil. This was an important concern when calculators were first becoming available in the early 1970s, and is an even more important and valid concern today in light of the well-known and well-publicized decline in computational skills of school-age children over the past several years. It is a concern that needs to be addressed, and one we will address in this chapter.

There are actually two different aspects to the question of calculator use vis-à-vis hand computational skills. First is the question of whether calculators are being made use of in place of teaching students to do arithmetic by hand and having them learn the basic number facts and skills. To this aspect of the question the answer, as we will see in the section on calculators in the elementary school, is a clear and emphatic "No." Calculators are definitely not either being used in the elementary school in place of the learning of basic arithmetic skills or being suggested for such use. On the contrary, virtually every article, position statement, conference report, and survey result dealing with the use of the calculator in the elementary school classroom makes an explicit point of the fact that students need to learn and master hand computation and develop the basic number facts and skills before being allowed to use calculators to do computational work. What we will see in the elementary school section of this chapter is that calculators are being used, and being recommended for use at the elementary level, as a means of *reinforcing* and *motivating* the learning of hand computation skills at the lower elementary level, and then to help in the development of higher skills like problem solving and pattern recognition at the upper elementary level or those students who have mastered paper and pencil computation. It is definitely *not* being employed to replace these basic skills and students are consequently *not* becoming dependent on these machines as computational crutches.

The second aspect of calculators vis-à-vis hand computational skills is, given that calculator usage is not replacing the learning of basic computational skills, is the availability of calculators helping to *improve* these skills and thus leading to a reversal of the trend of declining computational ability that has been in evidence for the past several years? This question will be looked at in depth in Chapter 3, where we will focus our attention on the vast amount of research that has been carried out at all grade levels on the effects of calculator use on both student achievement and student attitude. But we can give a preview of the general answer that we will obtain and that answer is "Yes," the use of calculators when employed appropriately and with care does in general result in improved achievement and in improved attitude both toward the learning of the particular subject being studied and toward learning in general. The availability of the calculator, far from replacing the learning of hand computation at the early school levels, is in fact *helping* to improve the learning of hand computation. Of course the effects of this usage will not be significant for several years since it is only those students who are using calculators from the elementary level on, and using them in appropriate ways and with appropriately developed material from competent teachers trained in calculator use, who will show the real effects in high school and college and beyond. Those students first being exposed to calculators in high school or at the college level and in a hit-or-miss fashion will not generally display these effects as significantly or as consistently since learning habits, skills, and attitudes are to a great extent determined in the first years of schooling, and their early training was not calculator oriented. But the outlook for those students who will be learning with calculators from the earliest grade levels on is for a fairly clear increase in both computational and some higher skills achievement and in the motivation to learn and to continue to learn.

Now let's talk about what we will be doing in this chapter and why. We will be taking a look at how calculators are actually being used, and the suggestions that are being made for their use, in today's schools at all levels from the elementary up through the college. We have two purposes in doing this. The first is to verify for you the claims we have just made about calculators not being used to replace the basic computational skills and concept developments but to enhance and reinforce them. The second purpose is to help you become a more aware and knowledgeable consumer in your child's calculator education so that you can better understand the ways in which the unique characteristics and benefits of calculators can and are being utilized in other schools, and better evaluate how well or badly your own child's school is taking advantage of these machines. If, after comparing the way your child's school is making use of the calculator's availability with the way other schools are making use of it, you have questions about it, you will have the necessary facts and information to try and influence a change in your school's approach to this new technology either individually or together with other interested parents through your parents' organization.

In reading this chapter keep in mind that what we will be describing is a compilation of activities being carried out, and suggestions being made, by many different teachers, administrators, and educational organizations. No one teacher or school is doing all the things with calculators that we will be discussing, even at any one particular grade level. The important point is that a large number of educators are doing *something* with calculators instead of ignoring them and hoping they will just go away. How calculators are used, when they are used, and the purposes for which they are used depend on individual teacher training in calculator use, department and school and parental support of calculator use, and school resources. So don't expect your child's school to be doing everything with calculators that we will describe. But they should be making some use of calculators consistent with their teachers' calculator interest and training and their students' capabilities.

One other thing to keep in mind is that, at the present time, calculator use is being done in a very ad hoc, individual teacher or individual school, manner. This means that there are no general national, or statewide, or even citywide topics or minimum competencies or guidelines for what teachers should teach students about calculators and what students should learn about calculators. Because of this it is somewhat difficult to talk about "how calculators are being used" at a particular grade level in the same way that we know we can talk about "what is being taught in algebra and geometry" in the high school. For algebra and geometry there are standard accepted curricula and textbooks and competency exams, but for calculator use no such standard curriculum or textbooks or exams exist, so it's pretty much dependent on what the individual teacher or school wants to do or not do. However, a fair degree of uniformity and consistency in calculator use has developed naturally over the years, and it is these consistent patterns and trends of calculator use that we will bring out and make explicit. We will do this by focusing one at a time on the following school levels: (i) elementary school, with sub-categories of lower elementary (kindergarten through 3rd grade) and upper elementary (4th grade through 6th grade); (ii) high school, with sub-categories of junior high (7th grade through 8th or 9th grade) and senior high (9th or 10th grade through 12th grade); and (iii) post-secondary school (beyond 12th grade starting at college).

THE ELEMENTARY SCHOOL—KINDERGARTEN THROUGH 6TH GRADE

From 1978 to 1980 the National Science Foundation (NSF) funded a series of conferences in Chicago and St. Louis for teachers, administrators, and parents on the subject of the classroom utilization of calculators. These conferences are described in the reports "Calculators in the Elementary School" and "The Calculator in the Classroom: Revolution or Revelation" (Leonard E. Etlinger and Earl J. Ogletree, NSF, January 1981). One of the activities carried out at these conferences was for the participants to form small working groups and to develop suggested guidelines for calculator usage in the schools. As detailed in the two reports mentioned above, the majority of the recommendations for the lower elementary level were for using the calculator to help students learn the basic number facts, concepts, and operations, and to reinforce this learning. For the upper elementary level the recommendations included continued reinforcing of these basic skills and the use of the calculator to allow students to deal with real-world problems like measurement, money, estimation, consumer education, and map skills that would make the material they learn more relevant and more interesting. It's clear from the recommendations given that the conference participants saw the calculator as a way to enhance the learning of basic computational skills rather than as a way of replacing these skills. This is brought out even more forcefully by the responses of over 400 conference participants to a series of questions on this matter. When asked "What grade levels are best suited for the use of calculators?", 55 percent of the respondents indicated that they thought elementary school an appropriate level as well as the higher levels. But when they were asked "Should children use calculators before they have mastered the basic facts?", 100 percent of the respondents said "No."

A more on-the-spot report of calculator use in the elementary school is given in the report *A Survey of Classroom Practices in Mathematics: Reports of First, Third, Fifth and Seventh Grade Teachers in Delaware, New Jersey, and Pennsylvania,* by A. O. Graeber and E. D. Rim (Philadelphia: Research for Better Schools, Inc., 1977). According to this report the most frequent uses of the calculator at the elementary level were drill, checking of answers, motivation, and remediation. At the higher grade levels calculators were also often used to help with word problems.

In a 1978 *State-of-the-Art Review on Calculators: Their Use in Education,* by Marilyn N. Suydam (Calculator Information Center, Ohio State University), a description is given of the four most common types of uses for calculators at the elementary level. These four uses are checking of pencil and paper computations, games, calculation, and exploratory activities.

As all of these recommendations and descriptions of calculator use indicate, students at the elementary level are still being taught to do arithmetic and to learn basic number facts using paper and pencil, with the calculator used at the lower elementary level for reinforcement, drill and practice, and motivation; and at the upper elementary level to reduce the computational load for those students who have mastered this skill and to allow them to spend more time on the development of higher levels of learning and concept development. There is just no evidence to indicate that *any* teachers are making use of calculators to replace the learning of hand computation. On the other hand, the availability of the calculator has also not resulted in some of the "revolutionary" changes in the elementary school curriculum that some zealous advocates of this new technology had predicted, at least not yet. This is clearly brought out in the article "Calculators" by J. Fred Weaver from the book *Mathematics Education Research: Implications for the 80's* (Association for Supervision and Curriculum Development, Alexandria, VA, 1981). After reviewing several studies of the way calculators are being used in the schools, Weaver concludes that very little in the way of revolutionary or innovative change has taken place in mathematics teaching that is due to the calculator, and expresses his "hope" that this will change in the future: "It really is not surprising to find that the most common uses of calculators are relatively pedestrian ones. This should change as teachers learn about and personally explore more significant roles for calculators."

Are we to believe, then, that because calculators have been integrated into the existing elementary classroom to be used with the standardly taught subject matter of elementary school rather than living up to the expectations some educators had for them in terms of causing "revolutionary changes" in the elementary school classroom, no benefits are being derived from their use? No, we should not believe this because it is simply not true. Weaver's description of present-day elementary school use of the calculator is very much an oversimplification and very misleading. True, the calculator has not caused a major revision of the elementary school curriculum. And, true, the recommendations made for calculator use at the elementary school level, as well as the descriptions of the topics that calculators are actually being used with and the purposes they are being used for, show that they are being applied to the same topics that were studied before calculators became available. But most educators and parents would agree that there is nothing seriously wrong with the topics contained in the current elementary school mathematics curriculum. What is wrong is that the students going through elementary school over the past several years simply haven't been learning these topics as well as they should. What the calculator offers is the opportunity to teach these important topics more effectively and carry through with this better and more successful learning to higher grade levels where the material learned in the elementary school is essential to the possibility of higher level learning. Certainly checking answers to arithmetic problems and learning about place value and estimation and pattern recognition were studied by elementary school students before the advent of the calculator. But the way they are being presented now with the calculator is very different, much more imaginative, and often much more successful in terms of achievement and motivation than before the calculator. This is what the calculator offers to the elementary school teacher and student and this is the kind of beneficial and successful change that is actually being experienced by elementary school teachers and students who are making appropriate use of the calculator. We will now describe several actual classroom activities that fall within the standard elementary school curriculum but which have been developed and used by educators specifically to make use of the unique characteristics of the calculator.

Checking Arithmetic Computations

In the article "Check Your Calculator Computations" (*The Arithmetic Teacher*, NCTM, December 1976), Charles D. Friesen provides a large number of arithmetic problems and shows how students can use their calculators to check the answers to these problems without waiting for the teacher's help and without the need for an "answer key." This not only frees the teacher from the need to waste valuable classroom time in merely checking individual answers, but allows the student to proceed at his/her own pace and to exert "control" over the activity by checking his/her own answers. The activity makes use of the fact that certain digits on a calculator's display resemble letters of the alphabet when the display is turned upside down. The arithmetic expressions that are selected for the activity all have answers that give a clearly recognizable word when the display is turned upside down, and each expression is accompanied by a clue as to what this word should be. To check an answer he/she gets on the calculator, the student simply turns the calculator upside down and looks to see if the display is showing a clear and recognizable word that fits the given clue. Some of the problems and clues from this article are provided below for your own amusement and so that you can see, when you try them on your calculator, that they really do allow you to check your answer.

Calculation	Numerical Answer	Clue	Word Answer
1. $(160 \times 5) + 7$	_____	A tennis shot	_____
2. $456 \times 81 - 1828$	_____	Capital of Idaho	_____
3. $394752 \div 512$	_____	Sick	_____
4. $706 - 99$	_____	A _____cabin	_____
5. $64118 - (80)^2$	_____	Letters that arrive near the first of the month	_____

Place Value

In the article "Instructional Games with Calculators" (*The Arithmetic Teacher*, NCTM, November 1976), Wallace Judd describes a game called *Wipeout* which teaches place value with the aid of a calculator and is appropriate for grades 2 and 3. The game requires two players. The first player takes a calculator and enters any three-digit number in which all the digits are different from each other (such as 271). The first player then passes the calculator to the second player and tells him/her which of the three digits in the display must be "wiped-out" or replaced by a zero. The "wipe-out" must be accomplished by one appropriate subtraction. For example, if the three-digit number entered is 271 and the 7 is to be wiped-out, the second player would have to realize that the digit 7 really represents 7 tens or 70 and to wipe-out the 7 (i.e., replace the 7 by a 0) requires subtracting 70 from the given 271. The answer, of course, would be 201 which has the same first and third digits as the original number but with the original 7 replaced by 0. Similarly, if the digit 2 is to be wiped-out then the second player must realize that the digit 2 in its given position really represents 2 hundreds or 200, and so to wipe it out it is necessary to subtract 200 from the given 271 and obtain 71.

Estimation

In the article "IDEAS" (*The Arithmetic Teacher*, NCTM, January 1979), Earl Ockenga and Joan Duea present classroom games that can be used with the calculator to improve student estimation skills in either addition, subtraction, multiplication, or division. The multiplication game is appropriate for grades 5 or 6 and is the one we will describe here. The students are divided into two teams (Team X and Team O) and are shown the game board illustrated in Figure 2.1. Team X begins by selecting any two of the available numbers and using its calculator to multiply the numbers together. If the product is on the game board an "X" is placed in that space; if the product is not on the game board no mark is placed. Team O goes now and in the same way selects any two available numbers, multiplies them together using its calculator, and places an "O" in the appropriate space if the product appears on the game board. The teams alternate turns, the winner being the first team to get a path of answers with their team mark on it connecting two sides of the game board.

While the teams may begin by selecting any two of the available numbers at random, they will soon discover that a better strategy is to locate the space on the game board where they would like to put their mark and then try to estimate which two available numbers will give the necessary value for that space as a product. Since none of the available numbers is a simple multiple of 5 or 10, it is difficult to multiply any two of them mentally and to determine the exact product before the formal selection is made. Instead, it is necessary to be able to estimate what the product might be and then see if this estimate is actually correct when the selection is made and the calculator is used to perform the multiplication. It is the availability of the calculator to

Ideas

Multiplication Game (2 teams)

How to play:
1. Teams take turns. Pick any two
   of these numbers.

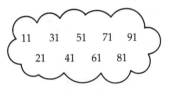

11 31 51 71 91

21 41 61 81

2. Multiply the numbers you picked.

3. Find the answer on the game board.
   Place your team's mark on it (X or O).

Game Board

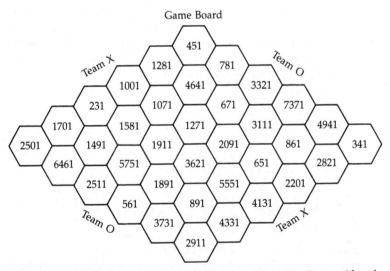

How to win: The first team to get a path of answers connecting its two sides of
the game board wins.

Figure 2.1

do the actual calculations that keeps the game moving and lets the players concentrate on the estimation and see immediately whether the estimation was correct. It is a learning game that loses much of its speed and appeal without the availability of a calculator.

Pattern Recognition

In Activity 1A, "The Jackpot," by Janet Morris (*How To Develop Problem Solving Using a Calculator*, NCTM, 1981), the student is asked to put himself/herself in the role of a contest winner who will be receiving for the next year (i.e. the next 365 days) $1 on the first day, $2 on the second day, $3 on the third day, up to $365 on the three hundred and sixty-fifth day. The student is asked how much money he/she will receive all together, and with the calculator available the first impulse is to simply start adding together all these individual amounts. However, this procedure is very slow even with the calculator used to do the addition since the student must still press all the keys. The activity sheet suggests instead that the student look at what the winnings will be for the first 3 days only, for the first 4 days only, and for the first 5 days only and try to discover a pattern that gives the result without having to directly add all the daily amounts together. The pattern the student is led to in this activity is illustrated below:

$$\text{First 3 days: } 1 + 2 + 3 = 6 = \frac{3 \times 4}{2}\,;$$

$$\text{First 4 days: } 1 + 2 + 3 + 4 = 10 = \frac{4 \times 5}{2}\,;$$

$$\text{First 5 days: } 1 + 2 + 3 + 4 + 5 = 15 = \frac{5 \times 6}{2}\,.$$

In other words, the result can be obtained by simply multiplying the last number in the list by a number 1 greater, and then dividing the product by 2.

Once this pattern is noticed, the student "verifies" it by using the calculator to find the winnings for the first 6 days, the first 7 days, and the first 8 days, first by simply adding up the values and then by using the discovered pattern and showing that the answers obtained both ways are the same. Finally, once the pattern and formula are verified to the student's satisfaction, the pattern can be used for the entire 365 days to discover that all together the student will receive a total of:

$$1 + 2 + 3 + \ldots + 364 + 365 = \frac{365 \times 366}{2} = \frac{133590}{2}$$

$$= 66795,$$

or $66,795.

Problem Solving

Problem solving is the process of applying previously acquired knowledge to new and unfamiliar situations. It requires reasoning, judgment, decision making, and often computation. Problem solving must be used when a situation is encountered for which we do not immediately know the answer or have a ready-made formula. Since real-world problems very infrequently occur in a form for which we have the immediate answer or an immediately applicable formula, practice in developing problem-solving skills is an essential part of schooling and, with the aid of the calculator, students can begin to develop this skill at the elementary school level.

In Activity 11, "Splash Time," from the book by Janet Morris on problem solving mentioned above, the student is told that membership in a particular swimming club is $5.00; that each individual swim for a member costs $0.25; and that each individual swim for a non-member who has not paid the membership fee is $0.75. The student is then led, through appropriate questions, to determine when, in terms of numbers of individual swims, it would be more economical to belong or not to belong to the swim club. This is done by using the calculator to fill in the following table:

Number of Swims	1	2	3	...	10	11	12
Member	$5.25	$5.50					
Non-Member	$0.75	$1.50					

From the completed chart it becomes clear that it pays to belong to the club only if you are going to go for a swim at least ten times. (This is true because it takes ten swims for the member to save the $5.00 membership fee with the lower member price for individual swims as opposed to the non-member price for individual swims.) While this activity could be done and the table completed without a calculator, it must be kept in mind that we are talking about elementary school students who need a great deal of time to perform hand computations. Using the calculator to help with the computations allows the students to concentrate on the problem rather than the computations and to learn useful problem-solving techniques like putting the information into a simple table to make it easier to understand and use. As simple an idea as the use of tables must be learned and a calculator activity like this one can help elementary students learn it without being unduly sidetracked by the computations involved.

Concept Development

In the bulletin *67 Ten-Minute Calculator Activities for Grades 4–8* (Calculator Information Center, Ohio State University, February 1981), Charles Thompson describes a calculator activity for helping students learn the relationship between multiplying or dividing a number by powers of ten and the movement of the decimal point in our base-ten number system. His technique involves having the student enter a number like 7 on the calculator and then repeatedly multiplying or dividing by 10 and noticing what happens to the decimal point after each operation. With a bit of guidance from the teacher when necessary the student can soon be led to discover that whenever a number is multiplied by 10 the decimal point moves one place to the right; and that whenever a number is divided by 10 the decimal point moves one place to the left. This discovery can then be generalized to other powers of ten by repeating the activity with 100 (10^2) and with 1000 (10^3). Understanding this seemingly simple relationship is extremely helpful in later mathematics and science courses where computation with decimals is employed and problems could be simplified enormously if the students simply had this relationship available to them and in mind.

These sample activities show not only how the special characteristics of calculators can be usefully integrated into the standard elementary school curriculum, they also show how the use of the calculator can make the learning of mathematics enjoyable and even fun. While the enjoyment of mathematics learning is not necessarily an end in itself, it is a welcome change of pace from the usual non-calculator student attitude toward mathematics and does increase the likelihood of more successful learning in mathematics and an increase in the student's desire to learn in general. For these reasons it is a benefit of calculator use that we should not overlook or ignore.

THE HIGH SCHOOL—7TH GRADE THROUGH 12TH GRADE

Calculator use in the high school classroom is in one sense very similar to calculator use in the elementary school, and in another sense is very different. Let's treat the similarity first. As we saw in the previous section, the availability of the calculator has not resulted in the kinds of major "revolutionary" changes in the elementary curriculum that some educators had predicted. Instead, the calculator has been integrated into the existing curriculum with its unique features and characteristics being used in innovative and imaginative ways to make the teaching of these standard, but still important, topics more effective and more long-lasting. According to Marilyn N. Suydam in *The Use of Calculators in Pre-College Education: Fourth Annual State-of-the-Art Review* (Calculator Information Center, Ohio State University, 1981), the same seems to be true at the high school level: "In few instances have calculators affected methodology—how mathematics is taught remains the same whether calculators are used or not, although the calculator can lead to differing teaching patterns and strategies."

Of course some changes are being made by individual teachers and will probably become commonly accepted in the near future with respect to topics that were either taught or dropped because of computational needs and limitations, since the computational realm is exactly where the calculator is most appropriate and most useful. For example, logarithms were originally developed for the sole purpose of simplifying complex computations. Since the calculator serves this same purpose much more easily and quickly, the topic of logarithms loses much of its appeal at the high school level. In fact, both the NCTM and MAA have recently recommended that the teaching of logarithms for computational purposes be dropped from the high school curriculum and it is quite likely that this will soon take place. (At the same time the topic of logarithms will probably remain in the college mathematics curriculum since it is used at that level for non-computational purposes such as studying the characteristics of special "functions.") On the other hand, the topic of continued fractions has many useful real-life applications but has dropped out of virtually every city and state high school mathematics curriculum because of the difficulty of evaluating and working with continued fractions by hand. With the calculator now available to simplify the necessary computations, this useful topic may begin to appear attractive once again and find its way back into the high school curriculum. All in all, however, this type of curriculum change is fairly minor and straightforward, and very little in the way of real change in the high school curriculum either has occurred up to now or is anticipated for the near future.

Now that we've mentioned the *similarity* between the high school and the elementary school levels in terms of the effects of calculator availability, let's turn to the *differences.* The major difference is that there is much more variety in the uses to which the calculator is being put at the high school level than at the elementary school level. One reason for this variety is the much wider range of needs and abilities that exists at the high school level. At the lower end of the spectrum are the students who never quite mastered the basic computational skills taught at the elementary level, and for whom the calculator can be used as an instructional aid to help in the remediation of these skills. An example of this use would be a one-quarter course offered by Don Fritz at the L. B. J. High School in Austin, Texas. This course was developed for remedial ninth-grade students who had not mastered the fundamental operations and has been in the school curriculum for over seven years.

A higher level use of the calculator is illustrated in the article "Why Not Have a Calculator Tournament?" by Larry F. Guthrie and Clyde A. Wiles (*The Arithmetic Teacher*, NCTM, November 1976). In this article the authors describe a calculator tournament that was sponsored by the Gary Area Council of Teachers of Mathematics and hosted on the campus of Indiana University Northwest, Gary, Indiana. One hundred twenty-eight students from twenty-eight schools participated in grades five through twelve with contestants competing against each other on specially developed problems with the aid of their calculators, and with all winners receiving awards.

A third specialized use of the calculator at the high school level, and one that is at the opposite end of the spectrum from its use in remediation, is illustrated in the article "A Summer Course with the TI 57 Programmable Calculator" by Eli Maor (*The Mathematics Teacher*, NCTM, February 1980). This article describes a special six-week summer course for advanced students in which students aged 8–11 and 12–15 used programmable calculators to investigate advanced mathematical questions and discover advanced mathematical ideas and concepts.

Another reason for the variety of uses to which the calculator is being put at the high school level is the fact that most high school students have already been exposed to calculators, and are somewhat familiar with their use, by the time they reach high school. This is indicated by the results of the mathematics portion of the National Assessment of Educational Progress (NAEP), a survey conducted in 1977–78 by the NCTM under a grant from the NSF. According to this report, 80 percent of the 13-year-olds and 85 percent of the 17-year-olds in the assessment stated that they had access to at least one calculator. The percentages are no doubt higher today. Consequently, while high school students may still have to be taught to use the calculator correctly and efficiently, it is not as new a machine to them as it is to the majority of elementary school students and they can therefore get right to using it and enjoying the fruits of its availability.

While the calculator is being employed at the high school level in a variety of ways for groups of students with special needs and special characteristics as illustrated above, its major use at this level remains as a teaching aid that is integrated into the standard high school curriculum. The difference here from the elementary school level is that the calculator's employment is used only minimally for computational purposes and most often for the development and enhancing of higher levels of understanding and concept development. These points are attested to and supported by three separate reports. First, in "Hand Calculators in Secondary Education: Evaluation, Analysis and Direction" by Wallace Fred Jewell, Jr. (doctoral dissertation completed in 1979 at the State University of New York at Buffalo), the author analyzes the calculator materials that have been developed for use at the high school level, the appropriateness of the high school curriculum for calculator integration, and the possible curriculum changes that calculator availability will have in the future. In the conclusions section of this study, he reports that his investigations show that "about half of the present high school mathematics curriculum supports calculator use of a substantive nature." Then, talking about the possibility of integrating the programmable calculator into the high school curriculum he says: "Programmable calculators have the potential to contribute significantly to the high school curriculum. These devices enhance many topics, particularly those related to number theory."

The second report is the bulletin *State-of-the-Art Review on Calculators: Their Use in Education* by Marilyn N. Suydam (Calculator Information Center, Ohio State University, 1978). This bulletin provides a list of the four dominant uses of calculators at the high school level. One of the four uses is with calculator-specific materials, and the statement is made that there is at least one text available that integrates the use of calculators into the standard curriculum subject matter, with several others being field-tested. Two of the other dominant uses are recreations and games, and exploration activities, with the following statement about calculator exploratory activities at the high school level: " ... because secondary school mathematics teachers' backgrounds are generally good *(i.e., since mathematics is their specialty),* there is much more of this type of activity than at the elementary school level. In addition, the students who continue in higher-level courses are often intrigued to explore."

The third report is given in the article "Calculators in the Elementary School: A Survey of How and Why," by Leonard E. Etlinger and Earl J. Ogletree mentioned earlier in this chapter as reporting on a series of NSF supported conferences on calculator use in the classroom. As we saw earlier, the majority of the recommendations for calculator use at the elementary school level made by working groups at these conferences involved using the calculator to help students learn the basic number facts and operations. At the high school level, however, the recommendations included reviewing concepts; creating math lab activities to reinforce concepts; promoting creativity in students to develop their own games and problems; solving statistical problems and their applications; aiding in the solution of real-life problems; and introducing programmable calculators to calculate commissions, mortgages, taxes, and interest.

The points being made by all three of these reports are that a large part of the high school curriculum is appropriate for substantive calculator use and the calculator is being used in these areas; that the calculator can be used, and is being used, to relate the mathematics covered in class to the situations and problems of the real world of the student to make it more meaningful and more useful; and that, while the calculator can and is being used at the high school level for helping students to develop their basic skills and computational abilities when appropriate, its most important and significant use at this level is in the development of higher level learning like creativity, concept acquisition and development, and self-guided exploration and discovery.

As we did in the section on the elementary school, we will now provide examples of actual classroom calculator activities that are appropriate for, and actually being used at, the high school level. We will do this by subject area such as algebra, trigonometry, and geometry since this is how most people think of the high school curriculum and how the subject matter of mathematics is usually broken down in most curriculums. At the same time we will try to give a variety of different types of activity including computation, tricks and games, and problem solving to show the different ways in which the calculator can be employed in each subject matter area. The calculator activities presented in this section are all taken from my recent book *Pushbutton Mathematics* (Prentice-Hall, Englewood Cliffs, New Jersey, 1982).

Elementary Algebra

Two important rules of arithmetic that students often have trouble remembering are that it is "illegal" to (i) divide any number by zero; or (ii) take the square root of a negative number. These rules are also important in algebra and the following calculator activity can help to remind students of them and give practice in being aware of the kinds of problems in which they play a part. To do this the teacher gives the class a problem like the one below:

Given the algebraic expression $\sqrt{5/s - 1}$. Use your calculator to evaluate this expression for each of the values $s = 0, 1, 5,$ and 7.5. If anything strange happens, redo the problem by hand with pencil and paper to discover what the difficulty is.

The calculator will display a perfectly good numerical answer when the values $s = 1$ or 5 are used, but will display an error message when $s = 0$ or 7.5 are used. When the student repeats these two values by hand he/she will discover that using $s = 0$ results in a division by zero and using $s = 7.5$ results in taking the square root of a negative number. The teacher can then remind the students that these are both illegal operations and that is why the calculator displayed an error message. A few additional problems of this type in class and in the homework will be all that's needed for the students to begin to be more aware of the possibility of these illegal operations and to be more careful in problems where they might occur.

Trigonometry

In this activity the class is divided into two teams, a calculator team and a non-calculator team. The teams then compete to see which one can more quickly solve one or more appropriate trigonometry problems given by the teacher. (Appropriate in the sense that the teacher knows the problems can be solved either with or without a calculator.) A problem I have used in this contest format is:

For the function $y = \sin(\phi)\cos(\phi)$, find the maximum value that y can take on for all values of ϕ between $0°$ and $360°$.

The most common calculator approach is to select a large number of values of ϕ in the given interval, use the trigonometric function keys on the calculator to evaluate the corresponding y value, and then use a table of these results or a graph based on them to guess the answer. An approach that can be used by the non-calculator team, and the one the teacher should hint at and encourage, is to use a substitution to simplify the given expression into a form from which the answer is immediately obvious. One such substitution that works in this problem is the well-known but frequently ignored "double angle formula for sine":

$\sin(2\phi) = 2\sin(\phi)\cos(\phi)$ for all ϕ.

Using this formula the given expression can be simplified to

$y = \sin(\phi)\cos(\phi) = 1/2\sin(2\phi),$

and since the maximum value the sine function takes on is 1, the maximum value the expression $1/2\sin(2\phi)$ takes on is $(1/2)(1) = 1/2 = 0.5$. After the problem has been solved, a member of each team explains how he/she obtained the answer so that the entire class can see both the calculator and non-calculator approach to the problem, and discuss the relative merits of each approach in this particular case. This contest format provides motivation and practice, and by alternating the teams everyone in the class gets valuable practice in the correct and appropriate use of the calculator.

Geometry

In this activity the students are led to discover, with the aid of their calculators, the property that the quotient of a circle's circumference C to its diameter D is always a constant, and the well-known formula that comes from this property for the circumference of a circle in terms of its radius R: $C = 2(Pi)(R)$.

The day before the activity is to take place the students are asked, as part of their homework assignment, to bring with them the next day several everyday circular objects from around their homes. When the students arrive with these circular objects they are instructed to use a ruler and string to measure both the circumference and the diameter of each object, and then to use their calculators to obtain the quotient C/D to several decimal places. When this is completed they are called by the teacher, one at a time, to go to the board and enter the values they obtained into the chart illustrated below:

Circumference (C)	Diameter (D)	Ratio = C/D

When the chart has been completely filled in, the students should be surprised to discover that all the ratio values are approximately the same, even to several decimal places. The teacher can then inform them that in fact the small differences in these values are due to the approximate nature of the circumference and diameter measurements and that, if all the measurements could have been done exactly, all the ratios would have been exactly the same. Furthermore, this common value of the ratios was first discovered over two thousand years ago by a Greek mathematician named Archimedes; it has an infinite decimal expansion that begins 3.14; and it is commonly referred to by the name "Pi." This discovery is then expressed mathematically as the relationship

$$C/D = \text{Pi},$$

which becomes

$$C = \text{Pi} \times D,$$

or

$$C = 2 \times \text{Pi} \times R$$

where R is the radius of the circle. This final form of the relationship is the well-known formula for the circumference of a circle in terms of its radius.

Intermediate-Advanced Algebra

One of the topics students in intermediate-advanced algebra sometimes have trouble with is that of zero and negative integer exponent notation. They have usually already learned what a positive integer exponent means and how to evaluate such an expression. For example, they would evaluate the expression $(2)^4$ by saying to themselves: "This means take the number 2 and multiply it by itself 4 times to obtain $(2)^4 = 2 \times 2 \times 2 \times 2 = 16$." One way of generalizing such expressions to zero and negative integer exponents is to give the class the table illustrated in Figure 2.2 and ask them to fill in the missing values above the dotted line.

$$2^5 = 32$$
$$2^4 = 16$$
$$2^3 =$$
$$2^2 =$$
$$2^1 =$$

. . . .

$$2^0 =$$
$$2^{-1} =$$
$$2^{-2} =$$
$$2^{-3} =$$

Figure 2.2

When this is done they are asked to use the exponent key on their calculators, $\boxed{x^y}$, to verify these values. They are then led to discover the relationship exhibited in this table that as the exponents on the left side of the equal signs decrease one unit at a time from 5 to 1, the corresponding values on the right side of the equal signs are obtained by successively dividing each value by two to obtain the next value. (Figure 2.3) They are now told to use this pattern to obtain the missing values below the dotted line (Figure 2.4) and then to verify the results with their calcu-

$$5 - 1 = 4 \quad \begin{cases} 2^5 = 32 \\ 2^4 = 16 \end{cases} \quad 32/2 = 16$$

$$4 - 1 = 3 \quad \begin{cases} \\ 2^3 = 8 \end{cases} \quad 16/2 = 8$$

$$3 - 1 = 2 \quad \begin{cases} \\ 2^2 = 4 \end{cases} \quad 8/2 = 4$$

$$2 - 1 = 1 \quad \begin{cases} \\ 2^1 = 2 \end{cases} \quad 4/2 = 2$$

Figure 2.3

$$2^1 = 2$$

· ·

$$2^0 = 2/2 = 1$$
$$2^{-1} = 1/2 = 0.5$$
$$2^{-2} = 0.5/2 = 0.25$$
$$2^{-3} = 0.25/2 = 0.125$$

Figure 2.4

lator using the exponent key $\boxed{x^y}$. Finally, they can be given the usual algebraic formulas for evaluating zero and negative integer exponential expressions and asked to use their calculators to verify that these formulas do indeed give the same values for the expressions below the dotted line that they found by continuing the numerical pattern. These formulas are:

$$a^0 = 1 \qquad \text{for } a \neq 0;$$

$$a^{-n} = 1/a^n \qquad \text{for } a \neq 0 \text{ and } n \text{ a positive integer.}$$

Business and Consumer Math

The aim of this activity is to allow the students to use their calculators to discover and verify several important properties about chain discounts; that is, situations in which two or more discounts in a row are given on the same item. To begin, they would be given a problem like the following:

A calculator costing $100 is being offered at a discount of 10%. After two weeks the price is further reduced by an additional 20%. What is the final price of the calculator and what single discount would have given the same final price as the chain 10%, 20%.

Using their calculators the students can easily discover that the first 10% discount reduces the price by (10%) ($100) = $10 down to $100 − $10 = $90; and the second discount further reduces this price by (20%) ($90) = $18 down to $90 − $18 = $72. Finally, the total discount is $28 which is equivalent to a simple 28% discount on the $100 item. The class would now be asked to redo the problem assuming that the discounts in the chain were reversed so that the 20% were given first and the 10% second, and should be surprised to discover that they get the same results for the chain 20%, 10% as they did for the chain 10%, 20%. This result leads to the hypothesis that perhaps the ordering of the individual discounts in a chain has no effect on the resulting single discount equivalent of the chain, which can then be verified by trying other examples on the calculator and finally proved by the teacher using algebraic representation. Other properties of chain discounts that the students can then explore, develop hypotheses about, verify by calculator, and then prove mathematically are that the single discount equivalent of a chain is always greater than any individual discount in the chain (the single discount equivalent 28% was greater than the individual discounts in the chain 10% and 20%), but always less than the simple sum of the individual discounts (28% was less than 10% + 20%). These are important properties for the students to be aware of since they can often be used to make quick estimates of the single discount equivalent of a chain for comparison shopping purposes when exact computation of the discount is not really necessary. The activity itself is also important because it shows that, while the calculator can be used in several examples to explore and try to obtain a pattern or a rule, and then on a few more examples to verify the rule to a certain extent, the only way to prove the rule for all cases is with mathematical theory. Thus, calculator exploration and mathematical proof go hand in hand and are not just equivalent alternative approaches to a problem.

Calculus

While this is a standard subject at the college level, it is also offered at many high schools for honors classes or for advanced students. The calculator is wonderfully suited to help students understand certain new concepts that are encountered in the calculus by letting them investigate these concepts in explicit and concrete numerical examples. An example of this would be the concept of the "sum" of an infinite series and its definition as a "limit" of the corresponding "partial sums."

Consider, for example, the expression

$$1 + 1/2 + 1/4 + 1/8 + 1/16 + \ldots$$

representing the "sum" of an infinite number of fractions. While it's obvious that you can never add together all of the terms in this series the way you can with a finite number of terms, a generalized "sum" can be defined in the following way. Call the ordinary sum of the first term S_1; the ordinary sum of the first two terms S_2; and in general the ordinary sum of the first n terms S_n. If these "partial sums" S_1, S_2, etc. get closer and closer to some fixed value S as n gets larger, then the original infinite series is said to have this value S as its "sum." (Figure 2.5)

$$S_1 = 1;$$
$$S_2 = 1 + 1/2;$$
$$S_3 = 1 + 1/2 + 1/4;$$
$$S_4 = 1 + 1/2 + 1/4 + 1/8;$$
$$S_5 = 1 + 1/2 + 1/4 + 1/8 + 1/16;$$

.
.
.

$$S = 1 + 1/2 + 1/4 + 1/8 + 1/16 + 1/32 + \ldots$$

Figure 2.5

Using the calculator the students should have no trouble obtaining the first ten or so partial sums and putting this data into a simple chart, although this would be quite cumbersome and prone to computational error if attempted by paper and pencil without a calculator. (Figure 2.6) It is now easy to see that the partial sums are getting closer and closer to 1.9999 . . . = 2 and so the sum of the infinite series is 2. This can now be followed by having the students calculate successive partial sums on their calculators without writing down the values by just adding on the next term each time. When this is done the successive digits can be seen to "click" into place in the display and remain fixed. That is, the first digit begins as a 1 and remains 1 from that point on; the second digit soon becomes a 9 and remains 9 from that point on; the third digit soon after that becomes a 9 and remains a 9 from that point on; etc. The partial sums can therefore be seen to fall into place giving the appropriate sum of the infinite series. This use of the calculator to illustrate new concepts by the use of concrete numerical examples embodying the concepts makes topics like this one much more understandable than having the students simply read about the material in the text or having them attempt to laboriously perform the computations with paper and pencil.

As this sampling of calculator activities shows, while the calculator is being applied predominantly to topics and problems that are a standard part of the high school curriculum, it would

Number of Terms (N)	Partial Sum (S_n)
1	1
2	1.5
3	1.75
4	1.875
5	1.9375
6	1.96875
7	1.984375
8	1.9921875
9	1.9960937
10	1.9980468

Figure 2.6

be misleading to think that this restricts the effectiveness or the innovative ways the calculator can and is being employed. It is a versatile and extremely helpful aid for improving the understanding of higher level concepts, for providing motivation, and for minimizing the computational drudgery that often interferes with continued learning for those who have already mastered paper and pencil computation.

COLLEGE LEVEL

Use of the calculator at the college level is very simple to describe. Essentially, aside from elementary courses where basic mathematical skills and hand computation are being taught to students who have never quite mastered them, there is very little restriction put on the calculator. It is being allowed in class, for homework, and often on tests.

The reasons for this liberal attitude toward calculator use at the college level are clear. First, it is pretty well accepted that students in college have already mastered paper and pencil computation, and pure computation is no longer the question; therefore, why not reduce the drudgery of computation in all aspects of college work including homework and testing and focus on the real higher level learning instead. (Keep in mind that for remedial math courses where paper and pencil computation is in fact one of the skills being taught, calculators are usually allowed for reinforcement and motivation the same way they are at the elementary and secondary levels for such purposes.) Second, even if these students might have some difficulty with paper and pencil computation, they will very shortly be finishing their formal schooling and going out into the business and professional world where they will be doing most of their computations with readily available calculators so they should have the opportunity to practice with these machines in their courses now. While most colleges and universities generally leave the decision to allow or not allow calculators up to the individual teacher instead of developing department-wide or school-wide policies, the consistent response of these teachers seems to be to place very few, if any, restrictions on calculator use in their classes. There is very little question that this will remain the educational level where calculators are most often and most widely employed, and where the most changes in curriculum or in approach will be felt.

CONCLUSION

We began this chapter with a brief discussion of the valid and important concern of many parents and educators about the possibly harmful effects of calculator availability, especially at the elementary school level, on students' learning of basic mathematical skills and ability to perform simple arithmetic computation.

The two aspects of this concern we focused on in this discussion were (i) whether calculators are being made use of in place of teaching students to do arithmetic by hand and having them learn the basic number facts and skills; and (ii) whether the availability of calculators can help to improve students' learning of basic arithmetic skills and thus help to reverse the trend of declining computational ability that has been in evidence over the past several years.

In this chapter we have answered the first of these two questions by showing that calculators have definitely not been used in either the elementary school or the high school to replace the learning of basic mathematical facts and hand computational skills. Quite the contrary, we have seen that at both of these levels the calculator has been integrated into the standard curriculum and is being made use of to enhance and reinforce the acquisition and development of these skills and to allow students who have mastered them to move on to higher level learning and concept development. For an answer to the second question we now turn, in Chapter 3, to a review of the literature dealing with the effects of calculator use on student achievement in, and student attitude toward, mathematics in particular and learning in general.

3

Research on the Use of Calculators in Education

In Chapters 1 and 2 we explicitly mentioned the fact that educators, as well as parents, have been concerned about the possibly detrimental effects of calculator use in the schools ever since these machines became generally available in the early 1970s. Partially as a result of this concern, the mid to late 1970s saw the publication of an enormous number of research studies on the subject of calculator use in the schools. This "explosion" of interest in, and research on, calculators was described by Marilyn N. Suydam in the 1979 publication *The Use of Calculators in Pre-College Education: A State-of-the-Art Review* (Calculator Information Center, Ohio State University): "Almost 100 studies on the effect of calculator use have been conducted during the past four or five years. This is more investigations than on almost any other topic or tool or technique for mathematics instruction during this century."

You might well think that with all this research data available, it would be an easy matter to answer virtually any question about the effects of calculator use on learning mathematics. This would be the case if all research studies were done well and reported completely and accurately, and if all such questions had one simple answer that held true for all students of a certain general type. Unfortunately, neither of these two requirements is generally true. For example, not all studies use enough subjects in their sample to make their conclusions validly applicable to a larger group, or run their studies for a long enough period of time for students to become used to and comfortable with their calculators and for any real calculator "effects" to become evident. Furthermore, not all studies use testing instruments that have been shown to satisfy the necessary characteristics of "validity" and "reliability" that all such good tests should exhibit. (*Validity* means that the test will actually be measuring what the researcher wants it to measure, not always a simple requirement when studying such categories of learning as concept development or problem-solving ability. *Reliability* means that the test will be consistent in the measurement it gives and not rate the same person highly one day and low the next day, or next week, on the same ability or task.)

In spite of the limitations and deficiencies of some of the research in this area, however, what we will find in our overview of the relevant material is that there is a common and consistent pattern of results that supports certain general conclusions. To give a quick preview, the consensus of the majority of research results will be that:

1. Students who learn with calculators in the elementary school almost always do just as well in paper and pencil computation as those who learn without calculators, and often do better.

2. Even though students who learn basic mathematics with a calculator can do paper and pencil computations quite well, they do even better and make fewer mistakes when allowed to continue to use calculators for computational purposes.

3. The use of the calculator in the learning of higher level skills such as concept development and problem solving is usually not detrimental and often facilitates this learning, although the results in this area are less conclusive and consistent than in the area of computation.

We will also look at some less formal, anecdotal descriptions and reports by classroom teachers and other involved educators of how calculators are actually being accepted by students and teachers, and the less tangible effects their availability is having on the classroom environment and atmosphere. These informal descriptions, together with the formal research results, will give us a well-rounded and complete picture of the measurable and non-measurable effects of the calculator's availability in the classroom. In particular, since the concerns we have mentioned are really related to the pre-college rather than to the college level, it is the elementary and secondary school research and reports upon which we will focus our attention.

Now that we have given a hint of what we will find, let's turn to the actual research dealing with calculator use in the schools.

THE EFFECT OF CALCULATOR USE ON HAND COMPUTATION

One of the earliest surveys of research on the effects of calculator use in the schools is the August 1977 report by Marilyn N. Suydam titled *Introduction to Research on Hand-Held Calculators, K-12* (Calculator Information Center, Ohio State University). From a list of twenty-eight research reports, some of them involving more than one hypothesis and corresponding data analysis, forty separate findings were noted and summarized. The results of this survey were that in 19 of the 40 cases (47.5 percent) the calculator group achieved significantly higher on paper-and-pencil tests (with which the calculator was not used); no significant differences were found in 18 of the 40 cases (45 percent); and in only 3 of the 40 cases (7.5 percent) was achievement significantly higher for the non-calculator group. Therefore, availability of the calculator did not in general have detrimental effects on the learning of and ability to do computations with pencil and paper, and often enhanced this learning.

The results of this 1977 survey were supported by additional studies conducted during the following two-year period. The results of these new studies were discussed once again by Marilyn N. Suydam in her 1979 report *The Use of Calculators in Pre-College Education: A State-of-the-Art Review* (Calculator Information Center, Ohio State University):

> Many of these studies had one goal: to ascertain whether or not the use of calculators would harm students' mathematical achievement. The answer continues to be "No." The calculator does not appear to affect achievement adversely. In all but a few instances, achievement scores are *as high or higher* when calculators are used for mathematics instruction (but not on tests) than when they are not used for instruction.

Further support for these conclusions is given in the article "The Impact of Electronic Calculators on Educational Performance" by D. M. Roberts (*Review of Educational Research* 50, 1980). In this article Roberts critically reviews eleven elementary and thirteen secondary level studies on the effects of calculator use and comes to the conclusion that 6 of the 11 studies at the elementary level (54.5 percent), and 6 of the 11 studies at the secondary level that involve computation (54.5 percent) show computational benefits due to calculator use.

One final piece of evidence on this question is given in the 1979 doctoral dissertation "Hand Calculators in Secondary Education: Evaluation, Analysis and Direction" by Wallace F. Jewell, Jr., discussed earlier in Chapter 2. Concerning research at the elementary level, Jewell says: "Numerous studies have been conducted on grade levels kindergarten through sixth grade, dating back to 1974. . . . A majority of the studies show significant gains with regard to achievement and learning concepts by the calculator groups." At the high school level, Jewell describes 13 major studies in which a calculator group was compared to a non-calculator group. He reports that in 6 of the 13 studies (46 percent) the calculator group did significantly better than the non-calculator group; in the other 7 of the 13 studies there was no significant difference between the calculator and non-calculator groups in achievement; and in none of the 13 studies did the non-calculator group do significantly better in achievement than the calculator group.

While the results of research studies on some questions are often vague or contradictory, there is nothing vague or contradictory about the results of the research presented in this section. For a variety of grade levels, for a wide range of geographical locations, and for students with varying characteristics of background and ability, the use of calculators in the learning of mathematics in most cases does not have detrimental effects on the students' learning of or ability to do hand computation, and in many cases actually results in increased hand computational achievement. In short, the concern of educators and parents that calculator availability would replace or harm the learning of paper and pencil computational skills have no foundation in fact and can be disposed of once and for all.

THE CALCULATOR AS A COMPUTATIONAL AID

The next question we want to examine is whether students who have learned their mathematics with the aid of the calculator can actually do computational mathematics better with the calculator than without. This is an important question because the learning of higher level mathematical concepts and skills often requires a considerable amount of computational work that needs to be done but that has no direct bearing on the real higher level learning that is taking place. If the student has mastered the basic computational skills, and the calculator can be used as a computational device effectively and efficiently to perform this necessary computational work, then the student's energy and concentration can be focused on the real learning aspects of the activity without being distracted by the accompanying computational drudgery.

Of course you would think that a student would be able, almost automatically, to do mathematical computation faster and more accurately with a calculator than without since the basic purpose of a calculator is to do computations. But this is not necessarily so since learning to use a calculator is a skill in itself and the calculator introduces many new possibilities for computational error that are not present when using only pencil and paper. Because of this it is necessary to determine whether or not students can adjust to these sometimes confusing machines and learn to use them to perform computations faster and more accurately than they can using only pencil and paper.

A major investigation into just this question was undertaken during 1977–78 as part of the *Second Mathematics Assessment of the National Assessment of Educational Progress* (NAEP, report available from the National Council of Teachers of Mathematics, Reston, VA). This study involved a sample of over 70,000 students across the country ages 9 years, 13 years, and 17 years; and one of the specific topics they focused on was the effect of calculator availability and use on achievement in a variety of areas including routine computational problems, non-routine computational problems, and higher-level skills like problem solving. One of the limitations of this study was that the subjects were given only fifteen minutes or so of instruction with their calculators and then told to use the calculators on the experimental problems provided whether or not they wanted to. Because of this, it is possible that the results comparing the calculator group with the non-calculator group might have been more favorable toward the calculator group if the students in this group had been instructed in the use of the calculator and given practice in its use over a reasonable period of time and in a planned format the way such instruction could be done in a classroom situation. In spite of this limitation, however, the results of the study in the category *Routine Computation* were extremely favorable toward the calculator group. These findings included:

1. Performance for 9-year-olds on simple addition exercises remained relatively consistent whether done with or without the aid of a calculator. Slight increases in performance on addition exercises were shown by 13- and 17-year-olds when a calculator was available.

2. Performance levels by all age groups on subtraction, multiplication, and division with whole numbers showed increases when a calculator was used.

3. Nine-year-olds' performance on subtraction, multiplication, and division computation with a calculator was only slightly lower than that of 13- and 17-year-olds without a calculator.

4. Thirteen- and 17-year-olds performed better on exercises involving decimals with the aid of a calculator than they did without a calculator.

Clearly, even with virtually no training or practice in calculator use, the availability of the calculator improved achievement in virtually all routine computational tasks and sometimes by quite a substantial amount.

The results for problems of *Nonroutine Computation* were not favorable to the calculator group, but this is understandable given the limitations of this study mentioned earlier. The problem is that these are exactly the kinds of calculator applications that require time and practice with the machine and its special operating characteristics, and the subjects in this study were given neither the necessary time nor the necessary instruction. Far from indicating that calculators cannot help in such non-routine problem situations, these results provide evidence that if students are to become effective and proficient in the use of calculators for more than routine computational purposes, they must be exposed to them, taught how to use them, and given practice in applying them to a variety of situations and problems. Clearly, such applications of the calculator must be learned, and the best place for them to be learned is in the schools from the elementary level on up.

Additional support for the conclusions given above from the *National Assessment* are provided in the publication *Impact of Calculators in Elementary School Mathematics. Final Report* by Grayson H. Wheatley and Richard J. Shumway (NSF, Washington, D.C., 1979). This report describes a year-long study in which two teachers from each of grades 2 through 6 from five Midwestern states participated (a total of 50 teachers). Some of the conclusions of this study were that: (i) there are no measurable detrimental effects for the first-year use of calculators for teaching mathematics in grades 2-6; (ii) children have a high, positive attitude toward using calculators in mathematics; and (iii) children can learn to use calculators for routine computational problems with only a minimal amount of instruction and can then perform these computations much more successfully than children not using calculators.

The results of these two major, multi-state studies clearly indicate that students who have learned mathematics with calculators can use their calculators to do basic routine computations faster and more accurately than students who do not use calculators. An inescapable conclusion of this is that once a student has mastered hand computation, he/she should be allowed to make use of the calculator to perform computations if this will help in the acquisition and development of supplementary and higher level concepts and skills. Furthermore, in order to be able to make use of their calculators in a variety of situations and for a variety of non-routine computational purposes, students need to be taught how to use their calculators and given extended and carefully supervised practice in its appropriate application.

THE EFFECT OF CALCULATOR USE ON NON-COMPUTATIONAL MATHEMATICS

The results of studies on the effects of calculator use on the ability to do non-computational mathematics and the acquisition of higher level concepts and skills are much more mixed; and it does not appear at this time that there is a single, simple answer to the question of whether calculator availability is beneficial, detrimental, or neither. For example, as mentioned in the last section, the 1977–78 NAEP study indicated that students who used calculators to do non-routine computation problems showed no improvement (although they also did not show any detrimental effects) over those students who did not use calculators. For problems in the category of *Concepts and Understanding*, however, the calculator results were generally negative. Typical of these results was the conclusion that "Thirteen- and 17-year-olds were unable to use a calculator to order a set of fractions between 0 and 1." On the other hand, there were both positive and negative results for problems in the category of *Problem Solving and Applications*, including: (i) Thirteen-year-olds using a calculator performed worse on 7 of the 10 exercises in this category than those given the same problems in paper/pencil booklets; but (ii) Seventeen-year-olds' performance with a calculator was better on 9 of the 14 exercises given in both calculator and paper/pencil formats.

Roberts, in the 1980 review of elementary and secondary level calculator research mentioned earlier in this chapter, also found the research results concerning non-computational mathematics inconclusive, as indicated by the following conclusion from that article:

> There seems to be little doubt about the computational value associated with calculator use. . . . However, [with respect to] conceptual and attitudinal impacts due to calculator use, there is less consensus as to what facts can be gleaned from the research literature.

Finally, in her August 1981 report *The Use of Calculators in Pre-College Education: Fourth Annual State-of-the-Art Review* (Calculator Information Center, Ohio State University), Marilyn N. Suydam gives the following summary of recent studies on the effects of calculator use on problem solving:

1. Calculators are useful for problem solving if the problems are within the range of students' paper-and-pencil computational ability (from a grade 4 study).

2. ... ...ackle difficult problems when using calculators (from a grade 4 study).

3. Students use more varied problem-solving strategies when using calculators (from a grade 6 study).

4. There is no significant difference in the number of problems completed with or without calculators (from a grade 8 study).

5. The use of calculators probably does not affect problem-solving scores significantly (from five different studies involving grades 3 through 8).

Thus, there is a great deal of inconsistency in the literature as to the effects of calculator use on the acquisition and development of non-computational mathematical concepts and skills. The inconsistency of these results most likely means that there is no one, simple answer to the question of how calculator use affects students' higher level learning. Under certain conditions and with certain types of students calculator use will be beneficial; under certain other conditions and with certain other types of students calculator use will not have any significant effect; and under still other conditions and with other types of students calculator use will be detrimental. It remains for continued research in the area to identify the students and conditions that constitute each of these three distinct situations so that they can either use or not use calculators in ways that will be most appropriate for them. But for now the question of how to identify the category a particular student fits into is still open.

INFORMAL DESCRIPTIONS OF CALCULATOR USE IN THE CLASSROOM

The effects of the introduction of calculators on the classroom environment is described in detail by Max S. Bell in the article "Calculators in Elementary Schools? Some Tentative Guidelines and Questions Based on Classroom Experience" (*The Arithmetic Teacher*, NCTM, November 1976). This article describes what took place when calculators were introduced into over twenty elementary and secondary classrooms, and it does so with a series of questions and answers based upon the experiences of the teachers in these classrooms. Some of the more interesting observations from this article are: (i) From the first grade on the children learned to use the calculators (usually within the first hour) with at most a worksheet and only a minimal amount of explicit instruction; (ii) there was almost invariably high initial interest, which persisted over a long time provided they were given interesting things to do with the calculators; and (iii) the children involved in this study did not become dependent on the calculators and rather quickly gained good judgment about doing easy things in their heads whenever possible instead of relying completely on their calculators for all computations.

Additional evidence of the benefits of calculator availability in both what students do and the classroom atmosphere in which they do it comes from the article "Using Hand-Held Calculators in Sixth-Grade Classes" by John J. Sullivan (*The Arithmetic Teacher*, NCTM, November 1976). This article describes a project organized and run by the Bureau of Mathematics Education of the New York State Education Department over an entire school year to investigate the effects of calculator use in sixth grade mathematics. Among the observations made in this article are that the use of the calculators caught the interest of the children and made the classes more fun; the children were encouraged to explore topics not usually studied intensively in sixth grade; and the use of the calculator to help with the necessary computations allowed the children to investigate practical topics such as compound interest that would ordinarily be out of bounds because of the computational complexity involved.

Finally, let us take a quote from Richard J. Shumway's "Response" to the article "Calculators" by J. Fred Weaver in the book *Mathematics Education Research: Implications for the 80's* (Association for Supervision and Curriculum Development, Alexandria, VA, 1981).

One of the most powerful and consistently reported effects of student use of calculators is the high enthusiasm and valuing students have for calculator-aided mathematics activities. Any device which causes so much pleasure to be associated with mathematics and increases the probability (that) appropriate mathematics strategies will be chosen for problem solving deserves special note.

As shown in the above reports and quote, the same benefits seem to come up over and over again whenever classroom teachers and other involved educators discuss the results of allowing calculator use in the classroom. These include increased student motivation and enthusiasm; reduced absenteeism and discipline problems; and the opportunity for students to work with more realistic problems and to explore and investigate problems and topics they would not be able to study without the availability of the calculator as a computational aid. This certainly seems to indicate that as long as the places where calculators are used and the ways in which calculators are used are determined and controlled by the teacher, the calculator seems to present us with a means of enlivening and enriching the classroom environment, and consequently making education both more enjoyable and more effective.

CONCLUSION

In this chapter we have surveyed the research literature on the effects of calculator use in the classroom including routine computation, non-routine computation, and the acquisition and development of higher level concepts and skills. We have also looked at reports of the effects of calculator availability on such less tangible aspects of the educational process as classroom atmosphere, student motivation, and the treatment of more realistic real-world problems in the classroom.

All of these findings, both formal and informal, seem to lead to the following conclusions: that calculators are not harmful; that they have many benefits to offer the educational process in general and the individual student in particular; and that there is every reason to continue to use calculators in the schools and to continue to investigate the best ways for making the most effective and long-lasting uses of them both for educational purposes while the student is in school, and for personal and professional uses after the student's schooling has been completed.

4

Special Calculator Features and Function Keys: What They Are, How They Work

In Chapter 1 we mentioned that while all calculators are essentially the same in the sense that they can all be used to perform the four basic arithmetic operations of addition, subtraction, multiplication, and division, they differ in a variety of other ways. Some of the ways in which they differ have to do with special features that affect the way the calculator operates. These special features are often mentioned in advertising, on the box the calculator comes in, and even on the calculator itself since they are meant to entice the potential buyer to purchase that calculator instead of some other that might not have such features. They include "automatic power-off," "continuous memory," "printing capability," and "solar cell power" in place of batteries.

Another way in which calculators differ from one another is in the large variety of special function keys that they may have. These include percent keys, memory and memory recall keys, reciprocal keys, parentheses keys, trigonometry keys, and keys for doing arithmetic with negative numbers. Logically, you would think that a calculator company would have a basic, inex-, pensive model with very few or no special keys to be used by students and others who only need to do simple arithmetic; slightly more expensive calculators with a few special keys that are the most often used for slightly more advanced computations; and much more expensive calculators with many specialized keys for advanced students and professionals who have learned how to handle a calculator well and use it for a variety of purposes. But calculator companies are not known for their logic, they are known for trying to entice people to buy their product. For this reason it is sometimes difficult to buy a calculator with a few special keys you want without also getting a lot of extra keys you do not really want and which will make learning to use the calculator more difficult than it really needs to be.

What we will do in this chapter is to describe and discuss those calculator features and special keys that are most common on the major, reliable brands of calculator, and that are most important for a parent to know about when selecting an appropriate calculator for a child to use in school or when helping a child to use his/her calculator on school work. In Chapter 5 we will use the information presented in this chapter to discuss the subjects and grade levels at which these special features and keys become necessary (or at least desirable) for doing classroom mathematics, and to develop a calculator buying guide chart based on grade level. Since the best way to learn about calculator special features and function keys is to actually try out what will be discussed in this chapter on a real, live calculator, get one or more to look at and use as you read through this chapter. This is not essential, but it will give you a better idea of what we are talking about than simply reading the chapter.

One final point before we begin our discussion and description. In order to make the use of certain keys and the operation of certain features more clear, we will make use of a simple notation that describes the keys that must be pressed on the calculator keyboard, and the order in which they must be pressed, to work out problems or to evaluate expressions. To illustrate this notation, suppose we are asked to add together the numbers 2 and 4 on the calculator. What we do is to write down the expression to be evaluated, 2 + 4, followed by a colon. We then follow the colon with the symbols for the calculator keys that must be pressed in the order in which they must be pressed. To make it clear that these symbols represent the keys they are placed within circles or squares to represent calculator keys, and this ordered sequence of "keystrokes" is called the "keystroke sequence" for evaluating the expression. Finally, the answer obtained in display when this keystroke sequence is pressed is sometimes placed within parentheses following the keystroke sequence. For the expression 2 + 4 this notation would look like

$$2 + 4: \boxed{2} \; \boxed{+} \; \boxed{4} \; \boxed{=} \; (= 6).$$

SPECIAL CALCULATOR FEATURES

Rechargeable versus Non-Rechargeable Batteries

With a rechargeable battery calculator, when the battery becomes weak and calculations either flicker in the display or disappear from the display completely, it is possible to connect the calculator to an electrical outlet for several hours using a "charger" that comes with the calculator. After an appropriate amount of time (as specified in the accompanying instruction book for the calculator), the battery will be recharged and the calculator once again ready for use. With a non-rechargeable battery, on the other hand, when the battery becomes weak or dies out completely, a new battery must be bought and the old battery replaced.

When hand-held calculators first came on the market there was in fact a distinct monetary advantage to buying a rechargeable calculator. Even though such a calculator cost more than a non-rechargeable one to begin with, the money to be saved by not having to buy replacement batteries would eventually make it a better value. There were and are, however, several disadvantages to having a rechargeable calculator.

First, the rechargeable battery is of necessity larger and heavier than a non-rechargeable battery. This makes the rechargeable calculator harder to carry conveniently. All those slim line calculators you see people using and putting into their shirt pockets are non-rechargeable since the rechargeable battery would require a much thicker case. Second, even though the battery in a rechargeable calculator can be recharged many times, even it will eventually die out and have to be replaced; and the price for replacing a rechargeable battery is often more than it would cost to buy a completely new non-rechargeable calculator. Third, if your child either forgets to plug in the rechargeable calculator to recharge it at night, or it does not get enough of a recharge, it will not function correctly the next day in school and your child will simply be without his/her calculator that day. (Most calculators do have what is called an "adapter," which we will discuss as the next feature, that allows the calculator to be plugged into an electrical outlet and used directly off of electrical current even if the battery is not working. But classrooms usually do not have too many electrical outlets, they are usually not located near the students' seats and their use would require the student to remain "attached" to the outlet. For these reasons the adapter is not really suited to classroom use, it is primarily suited to at-home use.) With a non-rechargeable calculator a student simply carries a replacement battery with him/her and, if the battery in the calculator seems to be getting weak, it can be removed and replaced. This requires no more skill than replacing the battery in a transistor radio or in a battery-powered wristwatch. Finally, many of the newer non-rechargeable calculators use a long-lasting cadmium or lithium battery that lasts over a year and costs only a few dollars to replace (like the batteries used in quartz wristwatches). My basic preference, because of its lightness and small size, is the non-rechargeable calculator with a long-lasting battery. But either the rechargeable or non-rechargeable is perfectly appropriate and good to use so if you find a calculator that has the other features and keys you want, and is large enough for easy handling and easy reading of the display, don't worry about which type it is.

Calculator Adapters

As mentioned previously, the adapter is a device that allows you to connect your calculator to an ordinary electrical outlet and run it directly from electrical current instead of using up the calculator's battery. Adapters are available for most, although not all, calculators. This includes both rechargeable and non-rechargeable models. In fact, the recharger and the adapter are usually the same piece of equipment on a rechargeable calculator, and as you use the adapter the calculator automatically recharges at the same time (although more slowly than if you did not use the calculator while you recharged it). For some calculators, for example, the majority of those sold by the Texas Instruments company (TI for short), the adapter comes with and is included in the purchase price of the machine. With many other calculators you have to ask specifically for an adapter and you must also pay extra for it, although the price is usually only about $5 or so.

An adapter is extremely useful for at-home work, such as homework or review of previously learned material involving numerical computation. With it, the calculator can simply be plugged into an electrical outlet and left on for as long as is necessary without either having constantly to turn the calculator off and on between problems, or running down the calculator's battery from overuse. An adapter is definitely worth having even if it does not come with the calculator and must be purchased separately. Keep in mind, however, that while the adapter for one calculator might fit another model or another brand, they usually are not interchangeable. So be sure to get the right one for your machine.

Automatic Power-Off or Automatic Shut-Off

The automatic power-off or shut-off feature was developed to save wear on the calculator's battery so that it will last longer and not have to be replaced as soon as would be the case without it. It is based on the discovery that it takes very little battery energy for a calculator to *do* arithmetic computations, but a great deal of energy simply to *display* the result. The automatic power-off or automatic shut-off feature commonly operates in the following way. When the calculator is on and has a value showing in display, if you do not press any additional calculator key within a certain amount of time (usually twenty or thirty seconds), the value will simply disappear from the display screen. The screen will then either appear blank, or have some type of display to tell the user it is waiting, such as a dot flashing back and forth across the screen. This saves the battery energy that would ordinarily be needed to keep displaying the value, but as soon as you are ready to continue and want the value back on the screen you have only to press the "equal" key, $\boxed{=}$, and it will reappear.

Keep in mind, however, that while this is how most calculators with this feature operate, some may operate differently and the only way to be sure with a particular machine is to either read its instruction booklet or to actually try this feature out. Consider, for example, my Casio fx-2700P programmable calculator. According to the instruction booklet that came with it, if a key is not pressed in six minutes the calculator will automatically shut itself off and any value in display will be lost. To my mind this is a less useful form of automatic power-off than the form that gives you back the number that was in display so that you can continue working with it.

The automatic power-off or shut-off feature that saves the number in display and gives it back to you on command is very valuable when, in the midst of a calculation, you need to stop and think before continuing. Instead of having to write down your intermediate result and turn the calculator off to save wear on the battery, or in cases where no paper is available simply turn the calculator off and resign yourself to doing the entire problem over again, the machine automatically "waits" for you to press the appropriate key to continue while it conserves its battery. This feature can also save you from discovering that when you put your calculator away yesterday you forgot to turn it off and so its battery is now completely dead. Of course, if you do not know that your calculator has this feature you might think it is malfunctioning when the screen goes blank, or simply not know how to get the screen working again without turning the calculator off and on and losing your previous work. If you know it has this feature, or you buy it specifically for this feature, it is certainly nice to have and I can think of no reason not to look for it if it can be obtained without having to give up some other desirable features or special function keys.

Continuous Memory

In a calculator, "memory" refers to one or more internal storage locations in which intermediate results of a computation can be "stored" for recall and use later in the computation. The actual keys and procedures used to put a value into memory and to recall it from memory will be described later in this chapter.

With most calculators, when you turn the machine off and then on again any values that had been in either the display or the memory have disappeared and you begin with zero in all places, essentially a clean slate. This was and is a nice feature and many calculator users come to think of turning the calculator off and then on as a quick and easy way to completely clear the calculator's display and memory before beginning a new problem. A few years ago several calculator companies began advertising a new feature on some of their calculator models that they called "continuous memory." If you have a calculator with continuous memory and you turn your calculator off with a value in one or more of its memory locations, the values will still be in those memory locations when you next turn the calculator on again. That is, a tiny bit of battery power is used, even when the calculator is turned off, to retain those values. The advantage of this feature, so the advertisements say, is that if you are using the calculator to do some important work and want to keep a record of the result, but you do not have paper and pencil handy to write the result down, you just put the result in memory and turn the calculator off. When you are ready to write it down or use it, you turn the calculator on again and recall it from memory. Another possible advantage of this continuous memory feature is that if you get an intermediate result and need to think things out before continuing your computation, you can save battery energy and still not lose the intermediate result by putting it into memory, turning the calculator off, and then turning the calculator on and recalling the value from memory when you are ready to continue. Of course, the common form of automatic power-off or shut-off feature also does this for you, and does it automatically.

The disadvantage of continuous memory is that what is in memory remains there when the calculator is turned off *whether you want it to remain there or not* (unless you specifically press certain keys to clear the memory before turning the calculator off). As mentioned previously, it was very handy, before this feature became available, to be able to clear both the display and any memories by simply turning the calculator off and then on again. With continuous memory you must either check the memory to make sure it only has zero in it, or specifically clear the memory with memory clear keys (to be discussed later in this chapter).

For example, the student who wants to use a memory location to add several values together, and who has forgotten that the memory already has a value in it from previous work, will have that extra value included in the new sum with a continuous memory calculator. All things considered, the continuous memory feature is often more trouble than it is worth to the novice or slightly-beyond-novice calculator user, and is just not worth either the extra cost or the trouble caused if the user forgets it is there.

Calculator Logic: What the Calculator Does with the Values You Give It

The major way in which calculators differ from one another is in their "logic of operation." This refers to how values have to be entered into the calculator to perform computations; the order in which the values have to be entered; and how the calculator operates on these values to obtain an answer. Since every calculator has one type of logic or another already built into it when it is manufactured, this is not really one of those features that you can either get or decide to do without. However, you can purchase a calculator with the particular *type* of logic you prefer if, after learning how they differ, you do indeed have a preference. Furthermore, since using a calculator in a manner inconsistent with its logic will lead the user to constant and serious computational errors, you and your child should at least be able to determine which logic a particular calculator uses and know how such a calculator must be employed. This is probably the feature with the greatest potential for error for the uninformed calculator user, so be sure you read this topic and understand it.

There are two basic kinds of calculator logic, and they are called *Reverse Polish Logic* (or RPL for short) and *Algebraic Logic.* Actually, there are two types of algebraic logic as well, although this is usually not explicitly mentioned in most calculator advertisements or instruction booklets, so I have given them the names *Left-to-Right Algebraic Logic* and *Hierarchy Algebraic Logic.* We will see shortly what these names refer to and why they were chosen. What we will do now is to describe these three types of calculator logic: in what ways they are different from one another, why one type might be more or less desirable than another for school-related work, and how to determine which type of logic a particular calculator has. Let us begin with the first mentioned, and *least useful*, logic: *reverse polish logic*.

A calculator with reverse polish logic is easily distinguishable because it does not have an equal key, $\boxed{=}$. This is because it does things "backwards" from the way we would ordinarily do arithmetic computation by hand. For example, suppose you simply want to add together the values 2 and 4 on the calculator to get the sum $2 + 4 = 6$. On a reverse polish logic calculator this would be accomplished using the following keystroke sequence.

$$2 + 4: \boxed{2} \ \boxed{ENTER} \ \boxed{4} \ \boxed{+} .$$

Notice that the first value in the problem, 2, is entered; then a special key is pressed which tells the calculator to remember this value (we have used the key $\boxed{ENTER}$ for this purpose since this is the key used on reverse polish logic calculators produced by the Hewlett-Packard Company); then the second value, 4, is entered; and finally the operation key $\boxed{+}$ is pressed. As soon as the operation key is pressed the answer, 6, appears in display. Notice that since there was no need for an equal key in the keystroke sequence, reverse polish logic calculators simply do not have the $\boxed{=}$ key.

While reverse polish logic can be a bit faster to use in complicated computations and will save time when a programmable calculator is involved, its advantage is really to the professional calculator user such as the engineer, economist, statistician, or mathematician. In fact, the major manufacturer of reverse polish logic calculators in this country, Hewlett-Packard (or HP for short), does appear from its advertisements to be aiming at this professional audience rather than at the casual calculator buyer and user. For schoolwork and school learning, however, it would be disastrous for a student to use such a calculator since its use is almost opposite to the way mathematical computation is learned and done by pencil and paper. In fact, a student who uses such a calculator would actually be learning two kinds of math: the way to do and think about math as it is presented by both teachers and textbooks and done by hand; and the way it needs to be done on a reverse polish logic calculator. What is really needed is a calculator on which computations are performed in a manner that parallels the way mathematics is taught and done in class and by hand so that it reinforces mathematical learning instead of opposing it. This is the case with either of the two types of algebraic logic that we will look at next, so be sure that your child has an algebraic logic, rather than a reverse polish logic, calculator. Since reverse polish logic calculators do not have an equal key, and algebraic logic calculators do, all you have to do is make sure your child's calculator has a key with nothing but

an equals sign on it, $\boxed{=}$.

With both types of algebraic logic calculators, simple arithmetic is performed on the calculator essentially just as it would be said, written or done by hand. For example, on an algebraic logic calculator the keystroke sequence for adding the values 2 and 4 would be

$$2 + 4: \boxed{2}\ \boxed{+}\ \boxed{4}\ \boxed{=} .$$

This keystroke sequence directly parallels the statement of the problem "two plus four equals," and so the calculator computation is reinforcing the arithmetic problem and how a student says or writes it. The difference between left-to-right algebraic logic and hierarchy algebraic logic occurs in certain types of mixed arithmetic expressions where more than one operation is involved.

Suppose, for example, your child is given the following arithmetic expression and asked to evaluate it:

$$1 + 2 \times 3.$$

Notice that this expression involves two arithmetic operations, addition and multiplication. If the student doing the computation were allowed simply to choose which of these two operations to perform first, there would be two different possible answers to the problem as illustrated below:

addition first: $1 + 2 \times 3 = 3 \times 3 = 9$;
multiplication first: $1 + 2 \times 3 = 1 + 6 = 7$.

In order to keep such a confusing and contradictory thing from happening, certain conventions have been adopted that tell a person, among other things, which of the basic four arithmetic operations comes first and which comes second when they both appear in the same arithmetic expression. This is called the "hierarchy, or ordering, of arithmetic operations." According to this hierarchy, multiplication should be performed before addition so the correct solution to the given problem is:

$$1 + 2 \times 3 = 1 + 6 = 7.$$

Now consider the student who was given this problem and who attempts to evaluate the expression on his/her calculator by pressing the calculator keys in exactly the order the operations appear as the expression is read from left to right. The keystroke sequence would be

$1 + 2 \times 3$: $\boxed{1}$ $\boxed{+}$ $\boxed{2}$ $\boxed{\times}$ $\boxed{3}$ $\boxed{=}$.

On what I have called a left-to-right algebraic logic calculator the operations would be performed just as the student entered them (just as they are written from left to right). This means the addition would incorrectly be performed first and the calculator would display the incorrect answer of 9. On what I have called a hierarchy algebraic logic calculator the calculator would automatically do the multiplication before the addition even though they were entered in the wrong ordering mathematically, and would then display the correct answer of 7. That is, a calculator with hierarchy logic has been internally programmed by the manufacturer to automatically wait when an arithmetic operation is entered and determine whether or not another operation is then entered that must be performed first. It has the hierarchy of arithmetic operations built into it.

The only major calculator company in this country that explicitly mentions and advertises some of its calculators as having hierarchy logic is Texas Instruments, and they refer to it by their own copyrighted name, *Algebraic Operating System* (or AOS). The majority of other calculator companies either do not differentiate between these two types of algebraic logic or use a variety of terms to talk about them that makes it difficult to know which logic a particular calculator brand and model has. Of course it is easy enough to tell which type of algebraic logic a given calculator has just by entering the keystroke sequence

$$\boxed{1}\ \boxed{+}\ \boxed{2}\ \boxed{\times}\ \boxed{3}\ \boxed{=}$$

and looking at the displayed result. If the correct answer of 7 is displayed, then that calculator has the hierarchy form of algebraic logic; and if the incorrect answer of 9 is displayed, then that calculator has the left-to-right form of algebraic logic.

Either type of algebraic logic is perfectly acceptable and useful for doing school related work both in the classroom and at home. The important thing is that the student know which type of logic his/her calculator has, and get practice in using it appropriately in mixed operation arithmetic, since using it as if it were a hierarchy logic calculator when it is actually a left-to-right logic calculator, or vice-versa, will cause repeated and possibly serious errors of computation. As long as the student does learn how to use his/her calculator appropriately, any arithmetic computational problem can be done correctly. As an illustration, the arithmetic expression 1 + 2 × 3 which we have used to show the difference between the two types of algebraic logic, would be performed on a left-to-right logic calculator as

$$1 + 2 \times 3 = 2 \times 3 + 1:$$

$$\boxed{2}\ \boxed{\times}\ \boxed{3}\ \boxed{+}\ \boxed{1}\ \boxed{=}\ (= 7).$$

Just make sure your child knows which type of calculator he/she is using, and gets practice in using it appropriately.

Error Messages

In mathematics there are certain operations or procedures that are considered "illegal," or mathematically unacceptable, in the sense that they do not give a finite, unique value as an answer. One of the simplest examples of this is division by zero. Although it is easy enough to write down the expression "1/0" if you don't care what this expression means, it really does not represent any finite real number. This is so because, if there were some number a for which $a = 1/0$, then it would have to be true that $a \times 0 = 1$. Since zero multiplied by any real number is zero, not 1, the number a we took to be the value of $1/0$ cannot exist. A similar argument could be used to show that no number can be divided by zero and give a unique, finite value as a result. For this reason, we say that "division by zero is an illegal operation."

When such illegal symbols or operations are encountered, the teacher or textbook usually warns the student about it, explains why it is illegal, and hopes the warning is remembered the next time this situation is encountered. It is helpful if the calculator a student is using to perform arithmetic computations also warns the student whenever such an illegal operation is attempted on the calculator, and most calculators do just this with an "error message." The error message is a symbol of some type that appears on the calculator's display and informs the user that something unacceptable has been attempted. While this is a welcome feature, there are three aspects of error messages that any calculator buyer or user should be aware of and we will describe these aspects here.

First, all calculators do not use the same error message, so the user must discover and become familiar with the particular error message his/her calculator employs. For example, the error message on the TI-30 is the word "Error"; on the Casio Memory-8F it is the letter "E"; on the Sharp Elsi Mate EL-502 it is the display "0.0.0.0.0.0.0.0"; and on the TI-57 programmable calculator it is a value, not always the same value, repeatedly blinking on and off.

Second, although virtually all calculators will give an error message for simple illegal operations such as dividing one by zero, they will not always give an error message for less common illegal operations. In fact, a calculator might appear to give an acceptable "answer" to a particular illegal operation it has not been prepared to detect and report, and if the student either did not know better or had not been warned about this in advance, he/she might think this illegal operation was allowed.

Third, there are times when a particular calculator may give an error message erroneously because of the way it has been designed to do computations rather than because the particular operation involved is illegal. For example, a section on exponentiation keys later in this chapter we will see that when most exponentiation keys are used with a zero or negative base, the calculator will display an error message. This is not because it is illegal to raise a zero or negative base to a power, but because most calculators do exponentiation by using logarithms and this method of doing the computation makes the calculator erroneously think the operation is illegal. This is another type of situation in which the student must be warned ahead of time so as not to be misled by the calculator's incorrect warning of an illegal operation.

The most direct way to get information about this feature on a particular calculator, aside from trying to find the information in an instruction book, is to actually try to do several of the more common illegal operations on your calculator and see what warning, if any, is given. To help you with this, a sampling of illegal operations is given below with their corresponding keystroke sequences. Since some of these will require special keys that might not be on your calculator, you may not be able to try them all. Just do those you can; identify your calculator's method of displaying an error message; and make sure it gives this error message clearly and consistently on all (or at least most) of the illegal operations listed below. Keep in mind that any illegal operation it does not warn your child about is an operation that may cause your child trouble when it is encountered in schoolwork and the calculator seems to be saying nothing is wrong while the teacher and textbook say something is wrong.

When trying out these illegal operations, keep in mind that when most calculators display an error message the display becomes frozen. To continue work or start a new problem after an error message you generally must either press the clear key or turn the calculator off and on again.

Examples of Illegal Operations 1. 1/0 (division by zero):

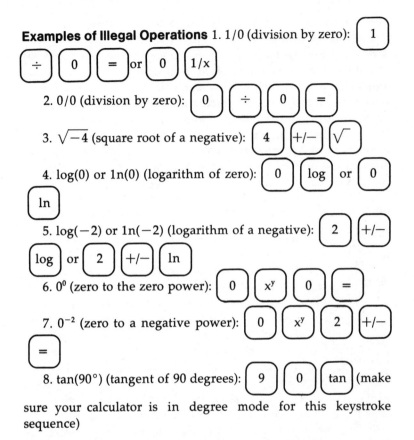

2. 0/0 (division by zero):

3. $\sqrt{-4}$ (square root of a negative):

4. log(0) or 1n(0) (logarithm of zero):

5. log(−2) or 1n(−2) (logarithm of a negative):

6. 0^0 (zero to the zero power):

7. 0^{-2} (zero to a negative power):

8. tan(90°) (tangent of 90 degrees): (make

sure your calculator is in degree mode for this keystroke sequence)

Scientific Display Capability (Scientific Notation)

Take a calculator, any calculator, and press the key with the digit five on it, [5] , until the display screen is as filled with fives as it can get. Now count the number of fives on the screen. That number of fives is called the "ordinary display capacity" of your calculator, so that if you counted eight fives we would say your calculator has "eight-digit display capacity."

While eight digits is quite a bit, suppose your child was doing a mathematics problem on the calculator in which the answer should be 156000000. (The calculator display does not show the commas that are usually employed when writing out large numbers by hand, so we will use that same convention and write 156000000 instead of 156,000,000.) Since this answer has nine digits it would be impossible to complete the problem and get the answer on an ordinary eight-digit display calculator. What would happen on such a calculator is that as soon as the computation produced an intermediate value that exceeded eight digits, the calculator's display would freeze or display some symbol, or do some combination of these things as described in the accompanying instruction booklet, to tell the user that it had reached its display limit and could go no further. The display could then be unfrozen by either turning the calculator off and on again, or pressing the equal key $\boxed{=}$ once or twice; but in any case the remainder of the problem would have to be done using pencil and paper.

While most problems in school would not require more than eight or so digits, there are exceptions to this (especially in high school physics and chemistry classes) and so it would be helpful to have a way of handling such extremely large values when they do occur. (In fact, even very small values may need more than eight digits to be represented, such as the decimal 0.00005555 . In this representation the decimal point does not take up a space in display but the five zeroes and the four fives would require nine spaces altogether.) The way this problem has been handled on many calculators is to make them automatically switch to "scientific notation form" in the display whenever the result of a computation requires more display space than the screen would ordinarily have. For example, consider the nine-digit number 156000000 mentioned previously. All you really need to describe this nine-digit number are the three digits 1 5 6 and some indication of how many zeroes to put after them. Scientific notation does essentially this. It takes the number and displays it, with a decimal point inserted, as a value between 1 and 10; then it tells you how many places to move the decimal point to get the true value. The number 1 5 6 0 0 0 0 0 0, for example, would be written in scientific notation form as

$$1.56 \times 10^8.$$

This means that to get the correct answer you must take the number 1.56 and move the decimal point 8 places to the right (putting in zeroes to mark any new positions). Doing this you would obtain the answer

$$1.56000000 = 156000000. = 156000000$$

8 places

On a calculator with scientific notation display capability this value would be displayed as

1.56   08,

which would similarly mean take the number 1.56 and move the decimal point 8 places to the right. The number 0.00005555 would, in a like manner, be displayed on a calculator with scientific notation display capability as

5.555   −05,

with the −05 at the extreme right telling you to take the decimal point in 5.555 and move it 5 places to the left to obtain

$$5.555 - 05 = 00000 5.555 = 0.00005555$$

5 places

In scientific notation, a *negative* sign in the two-digit number at the extreme right means the decimal point should be moved to the *left*, while a *positive* sign or the *lack* of a sign means the decimal point should be moved to the *right*.

While most calculators with automatic conversion to scientific notation mention this feature, it's possible one might not and you would like to be able to determine whether the feature is present or not. There is a simple way to do this. Just take the calculator and multiply the number 9 (or any other number greater than 1) by itself over and over again. If the calculator does not have automatic conversion to scientific notation display, then when one of your results gets large enough the display will simply freeze, or change to zero, or indicate an error message. If the calculator does have automatic conversion to scientific notation display, then when the results get large enough the display will suddenly switch to scientific form as illustrated above.

In addition to automatically converting to scientific notation display form when results of computations get either too large or too small for ordinary display, many calculators have special keys that allow numbers to be directly entered into the display in this form. This is very useful when the topic of scientific notation is itself being taught and studied, and the student must do arithmetic computation with numbers in this form. It is also useful when, in a physics or chemistry class, the numbers given in the textbook or as part of a homework assignment are given in this form. In the section of this chapter on special calculator function keys we will describe these keys and illustrate how they are employed.

The feature of automatic conversion to scientific notation, or even special scientific notation keys for that matter, is useful to have if the student is at a grade level where problems requiring this notation are studied or when the topic of scientific notation is itself studied. But it can be very distracting to a young student who really does not need this feature, and who is unaware of it, to be just fooling around with the calculator and suddenly have the display show something like 1.56 08 or 5.555 − 05 . So, if this feature is not really necessary, it is probably better to get a calculator that does not have it if that can be done without also having to give up some other desirable features and/or special function keys that you want. In Chapter 5 we will discuss the grade levels and subject areas for which this feature is useful and appropriate.

One final note regarding this feature. If your calculator does not have automatic conversion to scientific notation or scientific notation keys, then you simply cannot do arithmetic computation on it with numbers that are either too large or too small for ordinary display. This is one of the inherent and unavoidable limitations of calculator computation that must be faced and accepted when deciding whether or not to purchase a calculator with this feature.

The Shift Key Feature: More than One Function per Calculator Key

In the earliest hand-held electronic calculators each key on the keyboard served essentially one and only one purpose: a key represented one of the four basic arithmetic functions, or a decimal point, or a digit between 0 and 9, etc. A major limitation of this arrangement, of course, was that a calculator with only twenty keys was severely limited in the number of extra special functions it could provide. After all, the basic four arithmetic operations, plus decimal point, plus equal, plus digits from 0 to 9 already used up sixteen of these twenty keys. Of course in those days there weren't too many special functions anyway. Virtually the only ones available were the percent key, the square root key, the reciprocal key, and the memory and memory recall keys.

Someone then had the bright idea of increasing the number of available functions a calculator could provide by giving some or all of the keys on the keyboard multiple purpose capability, the same way each key on a typewriter's keyboard can serve more than one purpose (such as one key for both a lower case and an upper case "a"). On the typewriter, if you want the primary purpose of the key (such as a lower case "a") you just press the key directly; while if you want the secondary purpose of the key (such as an upper case "a"), you must press the "shift" key first. This is exactly what has now been introduced on many, perhaps the majority of, calculators in order to be able to provide a large number of special function keys on a small keyboard; and that is why I have referred to this feature as a "shift capability" and called the key that is used a "shift" key.

On a calculator with this feature each key has a primary purpose it serves, and that you will get when you simply press that key. This primary functional purpose is usually the symbol right on the key. The key may then also have a secondary functional purpose, and this would be given by a symbol either over or under the key, or in a different color to match the special color of the shift key. If you want this secondary function you must press the shift key followed immediately by the function key just as you would have to do to obtain an upper case letter on a typewriter. Some calculators even have two shift keys of different colors so that each function key on the keyboard can serve anywhere from one to three purposes.

Determining whether or not your calculator has the shift feature is quite simple. If every key has just one symbol on or near it (except for the clear key which may look like $\boxed{\text{c/ce}}$ or $\boxed{\text{on/c}}$ as will be discussed later in this chapter when "clear" keys are described), then the calculator most likely does not have the shift feature and should not have an easily recognizable shift key. If several of the keys do have more than one symbol on or near them, then the calculator most likely does have the shift feature and should have an easily recognizable shift key (usually in some obviously different color that matches the color of the secondary functions on or near the keys).

The most obvious advantage of this feature is that it increases the number of special functions that can be offered on a handheld calculator with a small keyboard. However, more is not always better and this larger number of special functions could be a disadvantage as well. Any extra key a calculator user must press to perform a computation is one more opportunity to make an error, and the shift key must be pressed every time you want to use the secondary function of a key instead of its primary function. Since there is always a chance of pressing the shift key by accident when it is not needed, or neglecting to press it when it is needed, the presence of this feature offers the potential of errors that does not exist when the feature is absent.

The best advice that can be given regarding this feature is the following. If you can get a calculator with the other features and special function keys you want without the necessity of a shift capability, then do so. If you must get a calculator with shift capability, try to get one for which most of the special functions you will need do not require the shift, i.e. they are the primary functions on their keys. This will minimize the use of the shift feature and the number of times its existence on the calculator might be responsible for an error.

Angular Measurement in Trigonometry: Degree Measure and Radian Measure

Trigonometry is first introduced to most students in school at the secondary level somewhere around the ninth or tenth grade, and it plays an important role in many of the later mathematical and scientific topics and courses the student meets. The essence of trigonometry is the study of geometric figures and the measurement of, and relationship between, the angles and sides of such figures. The difficulty with using a calculator to do trigonometric computations is that when angles are involved there are two different ways, or "modes," of measuring them, and both modes of measurement are taught and used in the development of the subject. The two modes of measurement are called "degree measure" and "radian measure." (There is a third mode or unit of measurement as well, called "gradient," but it is usually ignored so we will not discuss it here.)

The situation in trigonometry relative to these two modes of angular measurement can be compared to the situation of a carpenter who is building a house and working from plans which contain measurements given in both feet and inches. If the carpenter only has a ruler that is marked in feet, it is certainly possible to change all the inch measurements in the plans to equivalent measurements in feet and use this ruler to do all the measuring; and if the carpenter only has a ruler that is marked in inches, it is certainly possible to change all the foot measurements in the plans to equivalent measurements in inches and use this ruler to do all the measuring. But it is easier, and there is less chance of error, if the carpenter has both a ruler that measures in feet and a ruler that measures in inches, or one ruler that measures in both feet and inches. Similarly, there is a relationship between degree units and radian units that can be used to convert angular measure in degrees to an equivalent angular measure in radians, and vice-versa; and if you were simply *using* trigonometry you could switch all measurements to the one measure you have available although it would be easier and involve less chance of error if both modes of angular measurement were available on the one calculator that is being used. But in school-related work your child will not just be *using* trigonometry; he/she will be *learning* about it and learning about both methods of angular measurement as well as the relationships between them. This *will* involve both degree measure and radian measure and so it is almost essential that the calculator which will be used in the learning of trigonometry in the school have both types of measure.

How do you know whether or not a particular calculator has both degree and radian measure capability? First, this only matters if the calculator has keys for doing trigonometric computations since that is the only time the type of angular measure used makes a difference. The simplest and most direct way to tell if it is a trigonometric calculator and, if it is, whether it has both degree and radian measure, is to look through the accompanying instruction booklet. If that is unavailable, however, or if you do not have the time to search through the booklet, you can do it by simply inspecting the keys on the calculator. To be a trigonometric calculator, the machine must have one or more of the

following special trigonometric function keys: | sin | for "sine;"

| cos | for "cosine;" | tan | for "tangent;" | sec | for "secant;" | csc |

for "cosecant;" and | cot | for "cotangent." If it does have one or more of these keys then it is a trigonometric function calculator and has probably been set up by the manufacturer to work in one particular mode of angular measure whenever it is turned on. What you want to do now is look at the keyboard for a key or switch that would allow the calculator's user to switch from whatever measure it is in when it is turned on to the other mode. If a switching key or switch is provided, the calculator has both measures; if no switching key or switch is provided, the calculator does not have both measures since it can only work in the measure it is in when it is first turned on. The switching key or

keys or switch would be labelled by some symbol like | deg | for

"degree;" or | rad | for "radian;" or | dr | for "degree/radian;"

or some simple and easy to recognize variation of this. Keep in mind that when trigonometry is either being learned or used in schoolwork, as opposed to simply being used to solve problems away from school, both degree measure and radian measure are usually involved and so the trigonometric function calculator your child will be using should have both these measures on it.

Programmable Calculators

Suppose you have a problem in which the regular price of an item of clothing is given, and a certain sequence of arithmetic operations must be applied to this regular price to obtain a sale price. If you had to find the sale price for only one item of clothing, it would not be too difficult to use your calculator with an appropriate keystroke sequence to obtain a correct answer. Suppose, however, that you had to repeat this same keystroke sequence over and over to find the sale prices of five, ten or even twenty different items of clothing. It would certainly simplify your work if you could just have the calculator "remember" this keystroke sequence and then "play it back" automatically each time it was needed. This is just what a programmable calculator can do.

Having a programmable calculator remember a keystroke sequence that you enter by hand once is called "programming" the calculator, and having the calculator play back the keystroke sequence is called "running the program." The only limitations on programming a calculator are (i) the calculator can only remember a program that you enter by hand the first time, so you are limited in what you can program into the calculator by the functions that are available on the calculator's keyboard; and (ii) each programmable calculator has a maximum number of keystrokes it can remember (this is called its "program step capacity") and this limits the length and consequently the complexity of the programs that can be entered into the machine. Of course, by paying a higher price it is possible to get a programmable calculator with a large variety of special functions and a large program step capability.

Programmability is a fascinating and very useful feature in certain situations and for certain people. For example, to professional mathematicians, engineers, accountants, and economists who must repeat certain important computations over and over, it is a feature worth paying for and having. And it is very useful to teachers who must do a large number of similar problems when preparing lessons ahead of time or who must get the answers to large numbers of similar problems given in textbooks. It is also of use in many mathematics and mathematics-related college courses where students must repeatedly employ certain computational formulas over and over again that would be extremely time consuming and prone to error if they were done individually each time. For most students, however, especially those below the college level, there is no real need for this feature.

The majority of schoolwork simply does not involve the type of repetitive computation that would either make this feature worth paying for, or worth learning the often difficult methods of programming. Even when repetition is involved, it is probably involved expressly for the purpose of drilling the student in some important formula or procedure, and the effect of the drill would be lost if it were the calculator that was performing the repetition rather than the student. If a bright high school student is interested in this computer-like feature and wants to learn about it and use it for his/her own amusement and curiosity, by all means get him/her a calculator that is programmable in addition to having all the other features and special keys that are needed. Such a calculator can be purchased for as little as $35 or $45. (For example, Texas Instruments puts out several programmable calculators in this price range that are easy to use, come with an adapter, and include in the purchase price a very comprehensive and readable guide to learning how to program. Other companies also put out good, inexpensive programmable calculators, but Texas Instruments seems to have gone out of their way to make their calculators useful and understandable to the novice as opposed to putting out a fancy model for the advanced user that has lots of gimmicks and lots of extras.) But if the student really doesn't care about this feature, then stay away from it since all it does is make the calculator more complicated than is necessary. It is difficult enough to learn how to use an ordinary, non-programmable calculator without the added burden of trying to learn how to do programming as well.

Fractional Capability Calculators

One of the major objections to calculator use in the schools when they first became widely available was that they worked only with decimals and not at all with fractions. Since fractions themselves, and the relationship between fractions and decimals, is a major part of mathematics and mathematical learning, many educators feared that the use of calculators would have a disastrous effect on the place and importance of fractions in the school curriculum. As we saw in the chapter on how calculators are being used in the schools, and as some farsighted and informed mathematics educators predicted, this has not happened. Since the calculator is a tool to be used only when deemed appropriate, its availability and characteristics have not been the determining factors in what is taught and not taught in the mathematics classroom. However, some calculator companies have sought to provide fractional capability in a few of their calculator models and it is worthwhile to know which companies they are, how this feature is used and both its possible benefits and drawbacks.

The two companies that currently offer models with fractional capability, as far as I can determine, are Casio and Radio Shack. However, since these features are not in most cases being advertised explicitly any more, even the salesperson in the store may not know what you are talking about when you ask for this feature or just which models have it. You will most likely have to inspect the calculators' keyboards for a telltale key, or read through the accompanying instruction booklet to discover which have this feature and which do not. For illustrative purposes, we will describe the way this feature works, and the key that is used, on Casio models.

The fractional key on Casio calculators is $\boxed{a^b/_c}$. In order to enter a fraction such as 2/5 on such a calculator using this key, you would employ the keystroke sequence

$$2/5: \quad \boxed{2} \quad \boxed{a^b/_c} \quad \boxed{5}$$

and the screen would show "2 ⅃ 5." This symbol " ⅃ " is used to denote division since the ordinary division symbol is difficult to represent on most calculator display screens. You could now use this value in any type of computation on the calculator just as you can with any value entered as a decimal. While having a calculator capable of working with both fractions and decimals does at first glance appear to be useful in a classroom situation where both fractions and decimals are taught and used, there are nonetheless some major difficulties connected with it that must be recognized.

First, while fractions can be entered into the calculator's display as illustrated above, the calculator will display results in fractional form only as long as nothing but the four basic operations (addition, subtraction, multiplication, and division) are employed. As soon as any other operation key is used, such as reciprocal or square or square root, the display will automatically switch to decimal form. Second, when arithmetic operations are performed in fractional form the answer is always displayed in reduced form whether the user wants it that way or not. This means, for example, that when a student does the problem 1/4 + 1/4 by hand and obtains the answer 2/4, the calculator doing the same problem in fractional form will give the answer 1/2 since 1/2 is equivalent to 2/4 and is in lowest terms. This could be disturbing to the student who assumes, when the calculator answer does not look exactly like his/her answer, that he/she must have made a mistake. Even when the problem asks the student to express the answer in reduced form, the calculator gives the answer but does not show how the fraction 2/4 becomes 1/2. Therefore it does not help the student learn how a fraction is reduced or give reinforcement when the procedure is practiced. Finally, and most serious of all, is that very few teachers or students have, or are even aware of the existence of, calculators with this feature. This means the student with a fractional capability calculator will probably not be taught how to use it or given classroom or homework problems in which it is to be explicitly used to help learn about fractions and their properties. In fact, having a calculator with such capability and trying to use it without guidance may become more of a burden than a benefit. For all these reasons, it may be better to avoid this capability until the student is ready to learn to use it on his/her own. It is a helpful extra feature to have, but it is certainly not a necessity since it will probably not be explicitly used or mentioned by the teacher.

Solar Cell Powered Calculators

Several calculator companies now offer a calculator that has solar cells at the top or side of the calculator's metallic case. These solar cells convert light to energy and therefore do not depend on, and will never require the purchase of, batteries. These are perfectly good and dependable calculators and will indeed save you money in the long run as opposed to calculators which do require the periodic replacement of batteries. Actually, the savings of money is not that great since you can buy calculators that use long lasting batteries which last at least a year and cost only a few dollars to replace. So if you find a battery calculator that has more appropriate features and keys for your child than the solar calculators offer, it is certainly advisable to get the one with the battery. However, the solar cell calculator has the advantage that it cannot die out in class or in the middle of a computation due to a weak battery, and you do not have to carry around an extra battery all the time to protect against such an occurrence.

At the moment, solar cell calculators do not provide the same wide variety of features and keys that are available on standard battery calculators. However, as additional companies jump onto the solar cell calculator bandwagon, competition will result in as wide a variety and choice for solar cell calculators as currently exists for battery calculators. Even now you can probably obtain a solar cell calculator with many of the keys you want. For example, my Sears Model 711.58550 credit-card-size solar calculator has memory keys, a percent key, and a square root key. Before you purchase any solar cell calculator, however, there are three things you need to test regarding its operation.

First, you need to consider just *how much light* is required to power the solar cells so that the calculator can be used. It may be that in certain low-light conditions a battery operated calculator could be used and its display seen, but not enough light is available to power the solar cells on a particular solar calculator. To determine this it is essential that you try out the calculator, either in the store or around your home on a trial purchase, at varying levels of lighting so that you have a pretty good idea just how much light is needed for it to work. Second, you need to check whether the cells will be powered by all the different *types of lighting* you might want to use it in. For example, it might work with natural sunlight but not with artificial indoor lighting. Or, it might work both in natural sunlight and with incandescent light but not with fluorescent lighting. If this is the case, and you have bought it because it worked at home with lightbulbs, your child might take it to school where fluorescent lights are used and be unable to use it. Finally, suppose you are using such a calculator to figure out and balance your checking account (or your child is using it to do a problem at school and is in the middle of the problem). By accident you reach over the calculator to get a new pencil and your hand comes between the solar cells and the light source. As soon as the light source is blocked off will the calculator display either go blank or return to zero the way a battery operated calculator display would when its battery power is turned off? If so, then you have lost all the work up to that point and will have to redo the entire problem. You need to verify that covering the solar cells only briefly will not cause the display value and any values in memory to be lost, or you could have real troubles with that calculator.

On the two particular solar cell calculators I have used recently, the Sears Model 711.58550 and the Sharp Elsi Mate EL-826, all three of these possible defects in operation have been adequately protected against. For example, both calculators work well in both bright and fairly dim lighting; and they work equally well in both natural sunlight and different types of artificial light. Finally, the solar cells they use apparently retain some of the light they absorb as stored energy. This allows the display to retain values and remain in view even if the cells are fleetingly covered by accident. Only if the cells are covered for four or five seconds is the display lost and/or the calculator automatically shut off. It may be, however, that other solar calculators have not been so well designed and protected. So, by all means try out any solar cell calculator you may be thinking of buying to make sure none of the possible defects mentioned here exist. The main thing to keep in mind is that it is not worth the savings of a few dollars a year in batteries if there is even one feature or key you need that you cannot get in a solar calculator. You buy the calculator for its appropriateness, not because it has a fancy trick or feature or because it will save a few dollars a year.

Printing Calculators

Printing calculators are manufactured by virtually all companies that produce the standard non-printing type of calculator. They come with a small roll of paper or tape on which, if you press the appropriate key, the calculator will print the numbers and operation symbols as you perform arithmetic computations on the calculator.

This would appear at first glance to be a very desirable calculator feature. With it, the user could keep a written record of all computations and, if an error does occur so that an incorrect answer is obtained, the written record could be consulted to locate just where the error occurred. There is, however, one aspect of the operation of such calculators of which you should be aware and which makes this feature more suitable to the advanced calculator user rather than to the novice.

When the operations of multiplication or division are performed on a printing calculator, they are done essentially as they would be on a non-printing calculator or by hand. That is, if the multiplication 2 × 3 is to be performed, it would be done on the calculator using the keystroke sequence

$$2 \times 3: \quad \boxed{2} \quad \boxed{\times} \quad \boxed{3} \quad \boxed{=} \quad ;$$

and the answer, 6, would appear on the display. On the paper printout this would also be printed pretty much as it is given here. This is not the case, however, when the operations of addition and subtraction are involved. Printing calculators are really designed to be bought by, and used by, people who do a great deal of plain computation like accountants rather than by people who are learning to do mathematics and think mathematically like students. Therefore, they do not handle problems involving addition and subtraction the way it is handled on a non-printing calculator. We will illustrate this with the Sears Model 272.58200 printing calculator.

Suppose you want to do the simple subtraction problem 5 − 2 on this printing calculator. The calculator does not see this as a subtraction problem; instead it sees it as a problem in which the two values +5 and −2 are to be "summed up." In other words it treats the number 5 as an "asset" and the number 2 as a debit. The keystroke sequence this calculator requires in order to do this problem is

$$5 - 2: \boxed{5} \boxed{+} \boxed{2} \boxed{-} \boxed{T}.$$

The first value, 5, is entered followed by its sign $+$; and as soon as the sign key $\boxed{+}$ is pressed the calculator prints the number followed by its sign on one line of the paper. Then the second value, 2, is entered followed by its sign $-$; and as soon as the $\boxed{-}$ key is pressed the calculator prints the number followed by its sign on a second line of the paper. The key $\boxed{T}$ then asks the calculator for the "total," and at this time a third line is printed with the value of the total, 3, followed by the letter T. The printout for this simple subtraction problem would look like

$$5 +$$
$$2 -$$
$$3 \text{ T.}$$

This is fine for an accountant but not very useful in terms of paralleling the way subtraction is taught in class or done by hand. It is mathematically correct to think of subtraction as equivalent to adding signed numbers, but it is not very helpful in reinforcing the learning about subtraction that occurs in the classroom. Similar problems exist for addition problems on such a calculator or for problems involving repeated additions and subtractions.

The printing calculator seems to use a logic that is a cross between algebraic logic and reverse polish logic as described in an earlier part of this chapter. As such, it has the drawbacks associated with reverse polish logic and discussed at that time. Basically, this feature is only good to have for the student who has already become proficient with an ordinary, non-printing calculator. If the student then wants this record keeping capability and is able to learn how to use it, fine. But it would be a real hindrance to have this feature if the student is still learning how to use a calculator correctly and efficiently in the first place.

SPECIAL CALCULATOR KEYS

Arithmetic with Signed Numbers: The Negative Sign Key

The most essential special calculator key, and one that often does not appear on even the more expensive calculator models, is the negative sign key.

In mathematics the negative symbol has several uses. The first and most obvious is to denote the operation of subtraction, as in the expression "5 − 2." Another important use of this symbol is to denote the negative, or "opposite," of a positive number. An example of this second use would be in representing the temperature −10°C, which in some sense would be the opposite of the temperature 10°C. (Mathematically, −10 would be called the "additive inverse" of 10 since −10 and 10 add up to 0.)

The negative symbol key that appears on all calculators, $\boxed{-}$, is the key for subtraction only, *not* the key for representing the sign of a negative number. If it is inappropriately used for this latter purpose it may sometimes give a correct answer in arithmetic problems by accident, but it will usually either give an incorrect answer or cause the calculator to refuse to do the problem at all. As an example of this, consider the arithmetic problem $(-3) \times (-5)$ in which the negative number −3 is to be multiplied by the negative number −5. Mathematically, the correct answer should be 15 since $3 \times 5 = 15$ and the product of two negative numbers is a positive number. But if you try to perform this computation on the calculator using the subtraction key $\boxed{-}$ for negative signs you will not get this correct answer. The keystroke sequence would be

$$(-3) \times (-5): \boxed{-}\ \boxed{3}\ \boxed{\times}\ \boxed{-}\ \boxed{5}\ \boxed{=}$$

and what would most likely happen is that you would either obtain the incorrect answer −8 or your calculator would display an error message. The reason for this is that in the keystroke sequence the calculator sees both the keystrokes $\boxed{\times}$ and the second $\boxed{-}$ as operations, and most calculators are programmed to react in one of two ways when two operations keys are pressed in succession: (i) they assume the first operation was a mistake and the second operation is your correction; therefore they would ignore the multiplication and treat the problem instead as if it were $-3 - 5 = -8$. Or (ii) they assume there was supposed to be a number between the two operations and you simply forgot to put it in so they treat the given keystroke sequence as an error and display an error message. In either case the subtraction key $\boxed{-}$ has not served as a negative sign key and, in general, will not. What is needed is another key that really is a negative sign key and the two most common are the "plus/minus" key $\boxed{+/-}$ and the "change sign" key $\boxed{CHS}$. Both of these keys work the same way so we will illustrate with the $\boxed{+/-}$ key.

The $\boxed{+/-}$ key takes a non-zero value that is already in display and changes its sign. Thus, if the non-zero value in display has no sign (meaning it is non-negative), pressing the $\boxed{+/-}$ key will make a negative sign appear before it on the display. Similarly, if the non-zero value in display has a negative sign, pressing the $\boxed{+/-}$ key will remove the negative sign from the screen. Notice that this means the $\boxed{+/-}$ key must be pressed *after* the numeral it goes with has been entered. For example, the correct keystroke sequence to use with the $\boxed{+/-}$ in order to multiply -3 by -5 would be

$(-3) \times (-5)$: $\boxed{3}$ $\boxed{+/-}$ $\boxed{\times}$ $\boxed{5}$ $\boxed{+/-}$ $\boxed{=}$ $(= 15)$

and with this keystroke sequence you would obtain the correct answer, 15, in display.

This is an absolutely vital special key to have on a calculator once a student reaches the grade level where arithmetic computations will involve negative numbers as well as positive numbers. The exact level at which this occurs will be discussed in Chapter 5, but it does not hurt to be sure that *any* calculator you purchase for your child has this feature since its use in school cannot be overestimated.

Clear Keys

The basic use of a clear key is to get rid of an incorrect value that has been entered into the calculator's display, or to get the display ready for a new problem when a previous problem has been completed. Pressing the clear key simply returns the display to the value it has when the calculator is first turned on, zero.

What many calculator users may not be aware of is that there are actually two types of clear key provided on most calculator keyboards, and they are meant to serve two different purposes. Of course a person can use the calculator competently and correctly without ever knowing the difference between these keys, and many people do just this. However, since we are discussing special keys, we might just as well discuss these so that if a situation occurs in which having this information can save you time and effort, the information will be available.

To explain the difference between the two types of clear key, consider the simple arithmetic problem 2 + 4. On a calculator this could be computed using the keystroke sequence

$$2 + 4: \boxed{2} \; \boxed{+} \; \boxed{4} \; \boxed{=}$$

to obtain an answer of 6. If you actually do this on a calculator and look at the display at each step you will notice something interesting. When the first three keystrokes have been pressed,

and you are just about to press the $\boxed{=}$ key to get the answer, the second number 4 (the last "entry") is in the display but the first number 2 is not. Clearly, the number 2 is being remembered somewhere in the calculator or we would not obtain the correct answer of 6 when we pressed the ⎡ = ⎤ key. In fact, the first number you entered is being held and remembered in a special, temporary memory location that all calculators have for this purpose. The two types of clear key give you the option, at this point in the calculation, of either clearing only the last entry (the number now showing in display), 4, or clearing both the display value 4 and the first value 2 that is being held in temporary storage.

The three most common types of clear keys are ⎡ CE ⎤ , ⎡ AC ⎤ , and ⎡ C ⎤ or ⎡CLR⎤ . The ⎡ CE ⎤ key stands for "clear entry" and clears only the last entry, 4. The ⎡ AC ⎤ key stands for "all clear" and clears both the last entry, 4, and the value in temporary storage, 2. (In some calculators the ⎡ AC ⎤ key also clears any value in regular memory storage but this is unusual.) The ⎡ C ⎤ or ⎡CLR⎤ key stands for "clear" and, depending on the particular calculator being used, could clear either the last entry only or both entries. We will soon see how to determine just which of these two functions it serves on your calculator. First, let's illustrate the use of the ⎡ CE ⎤ and ⎡ AC ⎤ keys.

Suppose, in the keystroke sequence given earlier for evaluating 2 + 4, you discover just before pressing the final ⎡ = ⎤ key that instead of entering the correct second value 4, you accidentally entered the incorrect value 3. Your incomplete keystroke sequence would then look like

⎡ 2 ⎤ ⎡ + ⎤ ⎡ 3 ⎤

You can now use the ⏢ CE key to clear only the last, incorrect entry, 3, and replace it with the correct value of 4 before completing the computation with the ⏢ = key. The entire keystroke sequence with the incorrect value cleared and replaced by the correct value would be

$$2 + 4: \boxed{2} \quad \boxed{+} \quad \boxed{3} \quad \boxed{CE} \quad \boxed{4} \quad \boxed{=} \quad (= 6).$$

Corrects
3 to 4

If you had pressed the ⏢ AC key instead of the ⏢ CE , then both values 2 and 3 would have been lost and you would have had to do the entire keystroke sequence over.

To determine which function the ⏢ C or ⏢ CLR key serves on your calculator, simply use it in place of ⏢ CE in the keystroke sequence given above. If you obtain the correct answer of 6 then this key cleared only the last entry and is equivalent to the ⏢ CE key. If, on the other hand, you do not get the correct answer of 6, then this key cleared both values and is equivalent to the ⏢ AC key.

On some calculators two different clear symbols will appear on the same key, such as ⏢ CE/C . When a key like this appears on your calculator's keyboard it means that if you press the key once during a computation it will clear only the last entry, while if you press it twice in succession during a computation it will clear both the last entry and the value being held in temporary storage. To verify this, once again make use of the keystroke sequence.

$$\boxed{2}\ \boxed{+}\ \boxed{3}\ \boxed{CE}\ \boxed{4}\ \boxed{=}.$$

If you perform this keystroke sequence with the $\boxed{CE/C}$ key in place of the $\boxed{CE}$, you should get the correct answer 6 if you press $\boxed{CE/C}$ once but an incorrect answer if you press $\boxed{CE/C}$ twice in succession.

Of course, you can always use the $\boxed{AC}$ key or its equivalent when any part of a computation goes wrong and simply redo the entire problem without worrying about the distinction between the two different types of clear key. But in a long sequence of computations in which only the last entry is incorrect, this choice of clear keys could result in a great savings of time and energy.

Percent Key

The percent key, $\boxed{\%}$, is commonly found on both simple and complicated calculators. However, it is not always used the same way on all calculators. Some calculators, for example the Texas Instruments TI-30, allow you to convert a number given as a percent to an equivalent decimal expression simply by entering the percent expression and without even having to press the equal key. For example, to express 24% as a decimal on the TI-30 you simply enter this value as follows:

$$24\%:\ \boxed{2}\ \boxed{4}\ \boxed{\%}.$$

What will now appear in display is 0.24, the decimal equivalent of 24%. This is a very useful application of the percent key, but for some reason most calculators with a percent key will not do this for you. On these calculators, if you entered this keystroke sequence they would just ignore the percent and all you would see in display would be the number 24.

The most common use of the percent key, of course, is in multiplying a given value by a given percent to obtain, for example, the discount on an item that has been placed on sale. As an example, suppose a 24% discount is given on a $50 pair of designer jeans and we would like to determine the amount of money that will be saved as a result of the discount. Mathematically, we would simply multiply 24% by 50 or 50 by 24%, and one would think this could be performed on a calculator in either of the two ways

Percent First: [2] [4] [%] [×] [5] [0] [=] ,

or

Percent Last: [5] [0] [×] [2] [4] [%] [=] .

The TI-30 and some other calculators will, in fact, give the correct answer of 12 (i.e. $12) with either of these two keystroke sequence orderings. Most other calculators, however, will not. They will be set up to do such problems with their percent key only if it is given in one of these two orders, most commonly the ordering with the percent last. On the Casio Memory-8F and Casio ML-720 calculators, for example, if the keystroke sequence given above with the percent *first* is used, the calculator simply ignores the percent and multiplies 24 by 50 to get an answer of 1200. Only the percent-last order will work on these two calculators.

Since, mathematically, either ordering is acceptable, it would be helpful when buying a calculator with percent key to try out both of the keystroke sequence orderings given above and check that both give the correct answer of 12. If, however, you already have a calculator with percent key that only works one way, or you need to buy one like this for some other reason, make certain your child knows which order the calculator requires and has practice in doing percent problems that way. This will keep him/ her from making computational errors that are due to the way the calculator works rather than a misunderstanding of the mathematics involved.

Memory and Memory Recall Keys

There are occasions, in performing arithmetic computation on a calculator, when you obtain an intermediate value that you would like to save for later use. This capability is provided by memory and memory recall keys. On such a calculator one or more memory locations are provided into which this value can be placed, left, and then recalled when needed.

On some calculators, most notably those put out by Texas Instruments, the keys are given the names $\boxed{\text{STO}}$ for "store" and $\boxed{\text{RCL}}$ for "recall." On such a calculator, when you press the $\boxed{\text{STO}}$ key, the value that is in display at that moment will be put into the memory location and replace any other value that might already have been there. Actually, only a duplicate image of the displayed value goes into the memory location since the value also remains in display. Another key that does this same thing on other calculators is $\boxed{\text{Min}}$ for "into memory." When you want to get the value in memory back again you press the key $\boxed{\text{RCL}}$ for "recall," or $\boxed{\text{MR}}$, $\boxed{\text{MRC}}$ or $\boxed{\text{RC}}$ for "memory recall." A duplicate of the value from memory then appears in display, with the value still remaining in memory as well. On some Texas Instruments calculators more than one memory location may be given, such as the TI-57 programmable calculator which has eight memory locations numbered 0 through 7. To store and recall a value on a calculator like this, you would press the store or recall keys followed by the number of the specific memory you want to use. For example, storing a value in memory location 3 would require the keystrokes $\boxed{\text{STO}}$ $\boxed{3}$, and recalling a value from memory location 3 would require the keystrokes $\boxed{\text{RCL}}$ $\boxed{3}$. Other companies also manufacture calculators with more than one memory location and may have different procedures for storing or recalling data which would be described in their instruction books. Finally, all calculators with memory have special keys for clearing the memory location without affecting any other values. The most common keys used for this purpose are $\boxed{\text{MC}}$ or $\boxed{\text{CM}}$ for "clear memory." On a calculator without continuous memory, the memory can also be cleared by turning the calculator off and then on again.

In addition to the standard memory keys described above, many calculators have memory keys that allow you to do more than just "put a value into memory." For example, the $\boxed{\text{M+}}$ key takes the value in display and adds it onto whatever other value is already in the memory location instead of replacing that previous value by this new one. This "automatic addition" key is very useful when adding several values together since it relieves you of the need to press the addition key $\boxed{+}$ each time a new value is added on. For example, to add together the numbers 1 + 2 + 3 and recall the sum we would use the keystroke sequence

1 + 2 + 3: $\boxed{1}$ $\boxed{\text{M+}}$ $\boxed{2}$ $\boxed{\text{M+}}$ $\boxed{3}$ $\boxed{\text{M+}}$ $\boxed{\text{MR}}$

(= 6).

The sum which had been accumulated in memory, 1 + 2 + 3 = 6, would be recalled by the final keystroke in the sequence and appear in display. Of course you must be sure that the memory location starts out with zero in it by either turning the calculator off and then on if it does not have continuous memory, or pressing the appropriate "memory clear" key first. Otherwise, any value in memory from a previous problem will be included in this sum. Another key that automatically adds numbers together in memory is $\boxed{\text{SUM}}$.

Another special memory key is $\boxed{\text{M}-}$. This key takes whatever value is in display and subtracts it from what is currently in memory. For example, suppose you have been using your calculator to update your checking account by adding your previous balance and all deposits automatically in memory using the $\boxed{\text{M}+}$ key. You now come across a check which you have written for $50 and need to subtract this 50 from the amount in memory. You would simply enter 50 into display and press $\boxed{\text{M}-}$. This would subtract the displayed amount, 50, from the current value in memory.

All these memory keys, the basic "store" or "in memory" keys; the "automatic addition" and "automatic subtraction" keys; the "recall from memory" key; and the "clear memory" key are quite useful. Unfortunately, you cannot always get them all on the same calculator. For example, on the TI-30 you get "store," "recall," and "sum" for automatic addition but not automatic subtraction. On the Casio Memory-8F you get "memory recall," "automatic addition," and "automatic subtraction" but no simple "store" or "in memory." And on the Sharp Elsi Mate EL-502 you get "recall memory" and "automatic addition" but none of the other memory keys we have been describing. As long as you have some memory function keys, preferably at least the basic "store" and "recall" and "clear memory" or their equivalents, you can get along quite well.

One other feature related to calculator memory should be mentioned. On many calculators with memory a symbol appears in the display screen (such as the letter M all the way on the left) whenever some non-zero value is in memory, and disappears when the memory is cleared. This is a useful reminder to the user, especially on a continuous memory calculator where simply turning the calculator off will not automatically clear the memory. To determine whether or not a particular memory calculator has this warning, just put a non-zero value into memory and look at the display to see if any special symbol has appeared to acknowledge this use of the memory location.

Automatic Constant Key for Repeated Arithmetic

This key often looks like $\boxed{\text{K}}$ for "constant" since using the first letter of the word constant on the key, "C," would confuse it with the clear key. This key is used when one of the four basic arithmetic operations needs to be repeated several times with one of the numbers involved remaining constant throughout. (It may be the case, however, that a particular calculator may be programmed so that this automatic constant feature works only for some of the four operations and not for others. To determine if this is the case, either read the instruction book or try all four operations out to see which ones work and which ones do not.) As an illustration, you might want to multiply each of several different numbers by 10%; or you might want to add 15 to each number in a given list. This feature allows you to enter the value to be repeated each time and the operation to be repeated only once. The use of this key may be slightly different on different calculators, so we will illustrate with a very simple and inexpensive model, the TI-30 calculator which costs anywhere from $10 to $15.

Suppose you want to multiply the value 4 by each of the values 1, 2, 3, 4, and 5. In other words, you want 4×1; 4×2; 4×3; 4×4; and 4×5. You would perform the first multiplication on the calculator in the ordinary way, but with the automatic constant keystroke $\boxed{\text{K}}$ inserted just before the final $\boxed{=}$ key:

$$4 \times 1: \boxed{4}\ \boxed{\times}\ \boxed{1}\ \boxed{\text{K}}\ \boxed{=}\ .$$

The correct answer, 4, would now appear in display. The key $\boxed{\text{K}}$ in this sequence, however, has told the calculator that you want to do one or more additional problems in which the first value 4 and the operation × are to be repeated automatically. Therefore, all you have to do now for the remaining multiplications is to enter the second number and press the equal key and the calculator will automatically provide the first number and the operation. The complete computation for all five multiplications, with the results that would appear in display indicated, is:

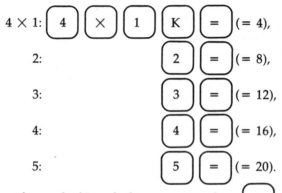

4 × 1: [4] [×] [1] [K] [=] (= 4),

2:                             [2] [=] (= 8),

3:                             [3] [=] (= 12),

4:                             [4] [=] (= 16),

5:                             [5] [=] (= 20).

Similarly, if you had used the operation key [+] in the

beginning of this keystroke sequence instead of [×] then

the calculator would automatically have repeated the operation of addition with 4 being added to each of the other values 1 through 5, respectively.

On some calculators with this feature, the key may have to be put at a different place in the initial keystroke sequence than as illustrated for the TI-30; or, as indicated earlier, it may only give repetition for some of the four arithmetic operations but not for others. Check the instruction book or try out various operations and sequences to determine just how your calculator uses this feature.

Exponent or Scientific Notation Keys

In the section on special calculator features we discussed the feature some calculators have of automatically switching their display to scientific notation form when the numbers involved in a computation get either too large or too small for ordinary display. As we mentioned at that time, many calculators also provide special keys that allow numbers to be entered directly into the display in this scientific notation form: that is, as a decimal value between 1 and 10 followed by a space, and then a two-digit number indicating how many places (and in which direction) the decimal point needs to be moved. This is done using the exponent key.

The two most common keys for scientific notation are $\boxed{\text{EXP}}$ for "exponent" and $\boxed{\text{EE}}$ for "enter exponent." Suppose, for example, we wanted to enter the scientific notation form number 5.555 07 into display. We would first enter the ordinary decimal part 5.555. We would then press the exponent key $\boxed{\text{EXP}}$ (or $\boxed{\text{EE}}$) to tell the calculator we are ready to give the two digit number on the right (the exponent). The display would show a space after the 5.555 and the two digits 00. If we now press $\boxed{7}$ we get exactly what we want. This is illustrated as

5.555 07: $\boxed{5}$ $\boxed{\cdot}$ $\boxed{5}$ $\boxed{5}$ $\boxed{5}$ $\boxed{\text{EXP}}$ $\boxed{7}$
(= 5.555 07).

If we had wanted to enter 5.555 −07 instead, to indicate that the decimal point is to be moved seven places to the left instead of to the right, we would just press the change sign key $\boxed{+/-}$ or $\boxed{\text{CHS}}$ after the $\boxed{7}$ to give the exponent a negative sign.

Once a number has been entered into the calculator's display in scientific notation form, it can be used in computations just as any ordinary display number can. Thus, to multiply the two numbers 1.25 02 and 2.5 01 together, we would use the keystroke sequence

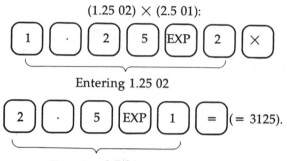

$$(1.25\ 02) \times (2.5\ 01):$$

Entering 1.25 02

Entering 2.5 01

All we have done is to multiply 125 (the value of 1.25 02) by 25 (the value of 2.5 01) to obtain an answer of 3125; but we have done it all on the calculator in scientific notation form. In this case it could equally well have been done in ordinary display form as 125 × 25. In cases where the numbers involved would be too large or too small for ordinary display, however, scientific notation would be the only way to do the computations on the calculator.

Exponentiation Keys: Raising a Number to a Power

The most common exponentiation keys are x^y and y^x. These keys are used when a number is to be raised to a power and are most often employed when the power (or exponent) is to be a positive integer.

To illustrate the use of this key, suppose we want to evaluate 2^5; that is, to find the value when the "base" 2 is multiplied by itself 5 times (5 is called the "power" or "exponent"). This could be done on a calculator directly as

$$2^5 = 2 \times 2 \times 2 \times 2 \times 2:$$

It is performed much more easily, however, with the aid of the exponentiation key using the keystroke sequence

$$2^5: \boxed{2} \boxed{x^y} \boxed{5} \boxed{=} \ (= 32).$$

In this keystroke sequence the base, 2, is entered first; then the $\boxed{x^y}$ key is pressed to tell the calculator that an exponentiation is required; then the second number, the power or exponent 5, is entered; and, finally, the $\boxed{=}$ key is pressed to obtain the answer. There are two things to note about the use of this key. First, the display may go blank for a second or two when the $\boxed{x^y}$ key is pressed. This just means the calculator is working, so don't enter the exponent until a value reappears on the display since the calculator will not accept any new values while it is working. Second, when a value does appear in display after pressing the exponentiation key, it may look like a very strange number that does not belong in the problem you are doing. Don't worry about that. It is most likely the logarithm of the base you entered since most calculators are designed to perform exponentiation by automatically transforming the problem to an equivalent logarithm problem. So don't worry about this strange looking value in display; just enter the exponent and press the equal key and if everything else has been done correctly you will be all right.

One word of caution concerning this common calculator practice of automatically (and internally) transforming exponentiation problems when the $\boxed{x^y}$ key is pressed into mathematically equivalent logarithm problems. Although it is perfectly legitimate and acceptable in mathematics to raise a negative base to a power, such as $(-2)^5$, such an exponentiation problem does not have an equivalent, legitimate logarithm transformation. This means that even though $(-2)^5 = (-2) \times (-2) \times (-2) \times$

$(-2) \times (-2) = -32$, if you try to use the keystroke sequence

$(-2)^5$: $\boxed{2}$ $\boxed{+/-}$ $\boxed{x^y}$ $\boxed{5}$ $\boxed{=}$

to evaluate this most calculators will display an error message to warn you that it cannot be done. In fact, these calculators would display an error message any time the exponentiation key is used with a negative or zero base. The student with such a calculator must be warned to disregard this particular error message and to use an alternate procedure to evaluate such expressions. This would be done by using the exponentiation key with the base as a non-negative value, and then supplying the negative sign if one is needed, according to the rules of multiplication, by hand when the answer is written down.

A final note. Some bases are used so often at different levels of mathematics that many calculators give a special exponentiation key, either in place of the general one we have described or in addition to it, already set up with that base. The two most common such bases are the number 10, and a constant value that has an infinite decimal expansion and so is usually denoted by the letter e (approximately 2.718 . . .). The special exponentiation keys for these two particular bases would be $\boxed{10^x}$ and $\boxed{e^x}$, respectively. To use these keys you simply enter the exponent (since the base is already part of the key), press the exponentiation key, and you will either get the answer immediately or you will need to press the equal key to finish off the calculation. You can find out in the instruction book whether or not the equal key is required for your particular machine.

Logarithm Keys

There are two distinct logarithm keys, and almost all calculators that give one of them give the other as well. The first is $\boxed{\log}$ and gives the logarithm of a positive number to the base 10. This is referred to as the "common" logarithm. The second is $\boxed{\ln}$ and gives the logarithm of a positive number to the base *e*, the infinite decimal mentioned in the last topic. This is referred to as the "natural" logarithm. Logarithm to the base 10 is more commonly encountered in lower level mathematics, such as in algebra courses at the high school level; while logarithm to the base *e* is more often employed in higher level mathematics, such as in a college level calculus course.

In simple terms, taking the logarithm of a positive number *x* to a base is the opposite of raising a number to that base as a power. This means, for example, that

$$y = \log x \qquad \text{if and only if} \qquad 10^y = x.$$

A similar relationship exists between the natural logarithm ln and raising the number *e* to a power. Therefore, asking for $y = \log 1000$ is the same as asking what power *y* the number 10 must be raised to in order to get 1000. The answer is 3, since $10^3 = 1000$ so $\log 1000 = 3$. To verify this on the calculator using the log key, use the keystroke sequence

$$\log 1000: \boxed{1} \; \boxed{0} \; \boxed{0} \; \boxed{0} \; \boxed{\log} \quad (= 3).$$

Notice that the number whose logarithm is to be found is entered first, and then the logarithm key is pressed. The answer appears in display without any need for the equal key. A similar keystroke sequence is used to evaluate ln of any positive value with the $\boxed{\ln}$ key.

Trigonometric Function Keys

In trigonometry there are six elementary trigonometric functions: sine (or sin); cosine (or cos); tangent (or tan): secant (or sec); cosecant (or csc); and cotangent (or cot). You would be hard pressed to find a calculator that gives keys for all six of these functions, but that is not really necessary anyway. The only really important keys to have are for the first three of these functions and these are $\boxed{\sin}$, $\boxed{\cos}$ and $\boxed{\tan}$. This is because the other three functions can be represented in terms of these three very easily and so most teachers and textbooks concentrate primarily on these three. In fact, some trigonometric calculators give only the [sin] and [cos] keys and leave out the [tan] key entirely since even tangent can be represented in terms of sine and cosine as tangent = sine/cosine. However, since all three of these elementary trigonometric functions are studied individually when trigonometry is taught, it is better to have a calculator with all three of the keys [sin] , [cos] , and [tan] if it is at all possible.

To use a trigonometric function key, the angle is entered first and then the appropriate function key is pressed. The answer will appear in display without the need for pressing the equal key. For example, suppose you want to evaluate the sine of 30 degrees: sin(30°). You would first make sure that your calculator was in degree mode so that when the value 30 is entered it is treated by the calculator as 30 degrees rather than as 30 radians or 30 of any other type of angular unit of measurement. (For a refresher on angular measure, see the topic "Angular Measurement in Trigonometry: Degree Measurement and Radian Measurement" presented earlier in this chapter.) You would now use the keystroke sequence

$$\sin(30°): \boxed{3} \ \boxed{0} \ \boxed{\sin} \ (= 0.5)$$

and the answer 0.5 would appear in display.

Parentheses Keys

Parentheses are used in mathematical expressions either to group terms that are supposed to go together, or to inform the reader that the ordinary hierarchy of arithmetic operations (which specifies which arithmetic operations are ordinarily performed before which others) is being superseded and altered in this particular situation. For example, consider the expression

$$(1 + 2) \times 3.$$

If the parentheses were missing, then the operation of multiplication would be performed before the operation of addition since, according to the hierarchy of arithmetic operations, this is the convention that has been adopted (see the topic "Calculator Logic" presented earlier in this chapter). However, the presence of the parentheses around the addition alerts us to the fact that in this special case the addition is intended to be performed first. Therefore, the expression should be evaluated as

$$(1 + 2) \times 3 = 3 \times 3 = 9.$$

The parentheses keys on a calculator, $\boxed{(}$ and $\boxed{)}$, allow you to evaluate expressions which involve parentheses exactly as they are given, symbol by symbol. On a calculator with parentheses keys the expression given here would be evaluated with the keystroke sequence

$(1 + 2) \times 3:$ $\boxed{(}$ $\boxed{1}$ $\boxed{+}$ $\boxed{2}$ $\boxed{)}$ $\boxed{\times}$ $\boxed{3}$ $\boxed{=}$

$(= 9)$

and would give the correct answer of 9 in display. Notice three things about the use of parentheses keys. First, as soon as the closing parenthesis key $\boxed{)}$ is pressed, the result of the addition inside the parentheses $(1 + 2 = 3)$ appears on the display. This means that you never need an equal key immediately after a close parenthesis key. However, when this intermediate value is then multiplied by another 3, the equal key is needed at the very end of the keystroke sequence. Second, parentheses never actually appear on the display screen. Only the numerical values appear, although some calculators do show on the display which of the operations is involved in a computation. Third, even if you do not have parentheses on your calculator you can evaluate an expression with parentheses; it just has to be done in an alternate way. The expression given here could be performed without parentheses keys in the following way.

$(1 + 2) \times 3:$ $\boxed{1}$ $\boxed{+}$ $\boxed{2}$ $\boxed{=}$ $\boxed{\times}$ $\boxed{3}$ $\boxed{=}$

$(= 9).$

The inclusion of the keystroke $\boxed{=}$ immediately after the addition part of the expression tells the calculator you want the
answer to the addition right then whether or not a higher order
operation is coming next. It is a very simple alternative to the
use of parentheses that works most of the time, and is one of
those tricks a student will pick up from simply using the calculator over a period of time on a variety of problems.

Parentheses keys are very useful so if you can get them, definitely do so. If you cannot, however, then don't be too concerned since, as illustrated above, alternative procedures can be
used to evaluate expressions without them.

Three Additional Special Calculator Keys

Three special function keys that tend to appear on almost any
calculator, and that are quite useful but usually not absolutely
essential to have, are the reciprocal key $\boxed{1/x}$; the square key
$\boxed{x^2}$; and the square root key $\boxed{\sqrt{x}}$. They work in the following way: (i) if a value a is in display and the reciprocal key
$\boxed{1/x}$ is pressed, a will immediately be replaced in display by $1/$
a. If a is zero, however, the calculator will simply display an
error message since division by zero is an illegal operation. (ii)
If a value a is in display and the square key $\boxed{x^2}$ is pressed, a
will immediately be replaced in display by a^2 (i.e. by $a \times a$). (iii)
If a value a is in display and the square root key $\boxed{\sqrt{x}}$ is pressed,
a will immediately be replaced by $\sqrt{a}$, a number with the property that if it is multiplied by itself the result is a. If a is negative,
however, the calculator will simply display an error message
since taking the square root of a negative number is an illegal
operation (i.e. a negative number cannot have a real square root
since no value when multiplied by itself can give a negative
answer).

Notice that none of these keys requires the pressing of an equal key. Furthermore, they can often be used in the midst of a chain of arithmetic operations without disturbing any previous computations. For example, the expression $1 + 3^2$ could be evaluated with the keystroke sequence

$$1 + 3^2: \boxed{1} \boxed{+} \boxed{3} \boxed{x^2} \boxed{=} (= 10).$$

The keystroke $\boxed{x^2}$ simply converts the number 3 (which is in display) to $3^2 = 9$ so that the computation becomes $1 + 9 = 10$.

5

Selecting a Calculator

In Chapter 4 we described and discussed the various features and special keys that comprise and are available on hand calculators. The purpose of that introduction was to acquaint you with what these features and keys are, how they work, and the options available within and between them. One of the major difficulties with the large number of features and keys that are available, however, and one we discussed briefly in that chapter, was that this wide choice sometimes makes it difficult to decide just which calculator to buy. Not only must you often give up certain features or keys to get certain others, you must often accept features and keys that you don't really want just to obtain certain ones that you definitely do need and want. As I said at the time, it would be much simpler if calculator companies simply made a basic machine with a low price, and then added on a few features or keys at a time at a slowly increasing price so that you could find essentially the kind of calculator you wanted somewhere between the simplest and the most complicated. Unfortunately, this is often not the case and so this chapter becomes a necessity as an aid in selecting the right calculator for your child's school needs.

There are really two conflicting demands that a calculator buyer faces. First, the need to obtain the keys and features that are really essential and helpful. Second, the need to keep away from keys and features that are not only unneeded but which could cause unnecessary errors or make the calculator more difficult to understand and use than it really needs to be for a certain level student or other user. Because of these conflicting demands, it is important in selecting a calculator to try to get the essential keys and features while avoiding the troublesome ones.

What we will do in this chapter is to go through the features and special keys presented in Chapter 4 very briefly, indicating the appropriateness or inappropriateness at different levels of schooling. We will decide into which of the usefulness categories each feature and key fit for the school levels lower elementary (Kindergarten through grade 3); upper elementary (grade 4 through grade 6); junior high (grade 7 through grade 8 or 9); senior high (grade 9 or 10 through grade 12); and college (beyond grade 12). The reason for choosing levels of schooling to look at in this way instead of individual grades is that there is great variation between what is taught at individual grades from one state to another, one city to another, and often even within the same city from one school district to another. By focusing on grade level categories instead of individual grades, we are able to reduce this variation considerably and make our discussion appropriate for and applicable to virtually all schools and students across the country.

After this brief discussion of the appropriateness of each feature and special key for the different school levels, we will provide a chart which gives a summary of our discussions in an easy to read and easy to use format that you can even take to a calculator store with you when you go shopping for a calculator. We will construct this chart by assigning numbers to represent the desirability or non-desirability of the particular feature or key for each level of schooling. Our numbering system will be: 1 = the feature or key is essential for this school level so make sure the calculator has it; 2 = the feature or key is not essential but would be useful for this school level so try to get it if you can without giving anything else essential up; 3 = the feature or key is neither excessively helpful nor harmful at this school level so take it if it comes with the calculator you want but don't worry if it's missing; 4 = the feature or key could lead to unintended errors or make using the calculator more difficult than it should be for a student at this school level, so try to avoid it unless you absolutely have to have it to get some essential other feature or key.

As you read the following discussions of features and special keys and their appropriateness for different school levels, keep the following two things in mind. First, the guiding thought in our rating scheme is to keep the machine as simple and uncomplicated as possible while still making sure it has all the features and keys necessary to do the required job at the intended level. Therefore, unless there is a real reason for having the particular feature or key, it will not get a rating of 1 and may not even get a rating of 2. The more unnecessary features and keys the calculator has the harder it is to learn how to use it; and, since calculators are so inexpensive there's nothing wrong with learning on a simple calculator and then proceeding at the appropriate time to a more sophisticated one. The second thing to remember is that the ratings I will give for each feature and key, and the reasons behind these ratings, are based on my own experiences and discussions with students, teachers, and parents. However, this does not mean that every one of my ratings is necessarily correct for every individual student with his or her own special capabilities and special needs. So use the given ratings as a guide, but if you feel that a particular rating is not really correct for your child and his/her particular school situation, don't hesitate to replace my rating with what you consider a more appropriate one and then use this modified rating chart to help you in buying an appropriate calculator. The important thing is to make sure the chart reflects as accurately as possible your situation and your needs. Now that we know what we want to do, let's get going with our brief look at the features and keys described in Chapter 4 and our development of a buying guide.

SELECTING SPECIAL CALCULATOR FEATURES AND KEYS

Rechargeability: As we indicated in Chapter 4, this is really a personal decision now that long-lasting non-rechargeable batteries are available at a relatively low price. Therefore, this feature gets a rating of 3 for all school levels.

Calculator Adapter: This feature is certainly not essential, but it can be useful when the calculator is being employed at home for a prolonged period of time and you don't want this extended use to wear the battery down. (Remember that even a recharge-able battery can eventually get worn down by continual recharging and have to be replaced at a not inconsiderable cost.) Since homework at the elementary level is usually not too time consuming, and much of the mathematics at the elementary level specifically aims at hand computation, we'll give a rating of 3 for the lower and upper elementary level. However, calculator use does expand and lengthen from junior high on, so for all these other higher school levels we'll give this feature a rating of 2.

Automatic Power-Off: This is a very useful feature at the lower levels where students may forget to turn their machines off and without such an automatic turn off feature the next time the student attempted to use the calculator the battery would be used up. At higher school levels where you can assume the student will not forget to turn the calculator off it is no longer essential, but it doesn't hurt to have the feature available. The cutoff is either the end of elementary school or the end of junior high school so to be safe we will give this feature a rating of 2 for lower elementary, upper elementary, and junior high; and a rating of 3 for senior high and college.

Continuous Memory: As we mentioned in Chapter 4, this feature can cause errors when a student forgets to explicitly "empty" the memory before making use of it to automatically add up values or use it for some other such purpose the way you can with calculators that do not have this feature and for which turning the calculator off automatically empties the memory. Furthermore, it is useful only in rare cases and for practiced calculator users. For these reasons we will give it a rating of 4 for lower and upper elementary school; a rating of 3 for junior and senior high school; and a rating of 2 only for college.

Hierarchy Algebraic Logic (as opposed to Left-to-Right Algebraic Logic): A student from junior high school on can learn, with a little practice, how to make perfectly good use of a calculator with either left-to-right algebraic logic or hierarchy algebraic logic, so there is really nothing but personal preference to use as a guide between them at these school levels. For this reason we will give this feature a rating of 3 for junior high, senior high, and college. For elementary school, however, students will tend to enter numbers as they occur in many situations and will be misled unless their calculator has hierarchy logic. For example, if the student tries to evaluate the following problem in addition of fractions using the indicated keystroke sequence, the correct answer will be obtained on a hierarchy logic calculator but not on a left-to-right logic calculator:

1/4 + 3/8: (1)(÷)(4)(+)(3)(÷)(8)(=).

The reason for this is that the hierarchy calculator will wait to perform the division in the second fraction 3/8 and then add this result to the first fraction 1/4, but the left-to-right calculator will perform the addition as soon as it is entered and therefore evaluate the given expression as if it were

$$(1/4 + 3) - 8$$

instead of

$$1/4 + 3/8 .$$

Therefore, because of the particular uses the calculator is put to in elementary school, it is useful although not essential to have a hierarchy algebraic logic calculator and we therefore assign a rating of 2 to this feature for lower and upper elementary school.

Clear "Error Messages" When Appropriate: From the earliest use of the calculator on, it is important that when illegal keys are pressed or illegal operations attempted the calculator display a clear, understandable message to this effect. For this reason we are assigning a rating of 1 to this feature for every school level. Of course, the specific types of errors that might be made differ at each level so the simple calculator for elementary school use will not have as many illegal operations to be concerned about (since it will not have as many special purpose keys) as a calculator for higher level use. Clear and appropriate error messages are important if a student is to learn how to use the calculator well and efficiently so this is an important feature to be concerned about.

Scientific Display Capability and Scientific Display Keys: Scientific display is not needed at the elementary level and could even be confusing to an elementary school student if such a display should suddenly appear on the screen by accident. For this reason we will give this feature a rating of 4 for lower and upper elementary school. At the junior high level it is useful to have since some teachers may introduce scientific notation, and even if it simply occurs in the calculator display by accident the teacher should be able to explain what this strange display means and the student should be experienced enough to understand and even enjoy using it. Therefore, at the junior high schol level we give it a rating of 3. For senior high school and college it is almost a necessity since this notation is frequently made use of in math and science and related courses, so here we give it a rating of 1.

Shift Feature: For the elementary school level you should be able to obtain all the keys you want and need without need for a shift feature. In addition, this feature may make the calculator a bit too complicated for an elementary school student to use. Therefore, it receives a rating of 4 from us for both the lower and upper elementary school level. From junior high school on up the students should be able to handle the use of this feature with practice, and it becomes almost a necessity in order for the calculator keyboard to be able to accommodate the extra keys that are appropriate for these higher levels. Therefore, for junior high, senior high, and college, we give it a rating of 3. If you can get what you want without it, fine; otherwise, take the feature and don't worry too much about it.

Trigonometry Keys and Degree and Radian Keys: Trigonometry is generally first encountered at the senior high level, although it could be encountered at the junior high level as well. Once the subject is reached and begins to be studied the student really must have these keys and capabilities, so we will give them a rating of 1 for college and senior high school, a rating of 2 for junior high school, and a rating of 4 for elementary school since at these low levels they are not needed and will do nothing but confuse the student who accidentally uses them or wonders about them.

Programmability: Without question, this capability is out of place at the elementary school levels and so it gets a rating of 4 there. For the junior and senior high school levels it is very dependent upon the interest and capability of the individual student as to whether it will or will not be helpful, so the rating at these levels is 3. At the college level it is not essential but is definitely useful for the student who wants it and cares to learn to use it so a rating of 2 at the college level seems about right.

Fractional Capability: Since only very few calculators have this capability, most students and teachers will not even be aware of it and will most likely not use this calculator feature in the classroom. This leaves it to the individual student who has this capability to learn about it and use it at appropriate times. Because of this reliance upon the student to learn to use it, but the low probability that it would be explicitly taught or used in the classroom, we give it a rating of 4 for the elementary levels, a rating of 3 for the high school levels, and a rating of 2 for the college level where a student could make better and more appropriate use of it.

Solar Cell Power: As we mentioned in Chapter 4, solar cell power has the advantage of your never having to replace a battery or worrying that the battery will die when you most need it. On the other hand, the variety of keys and features currently available on these calculators does not compare with that available on regular battery powered calculators. If you can find the kind of features and keys you want on a solar cell calculator, fine; if not, don't worry about it. For this reason, we give this feature a rating of 3 for all school levels.

Printing Capability: Because of the difficulties involved in performing computations with such a calculator, as discussed and described in Chapter 4, this feature might prove somewhat troublesome for most students. Therefore, we give it a rating of 4 for lower elementary school up through senior high school. At the college level the student should be able to handle its operation, and it is possible that having a printed record of the computations that have been performed could be desirable. It all depends on the needs and capabilities of the individual student so we will give it a rating of 3 for the college level.

Plus/Minus or Change Sign Key: This is the key that is used to enter negative numbers into the calculator for computation with signed numbers. Since negative numbers within computations are not ordinarily dealt with until the upper elementary school level this key does not become essential until then. However, it does not hurt to have it on any calculator for any level so we will give it a desirable rating of 2 for lower elementary school and an essential rating of 1 for all higher levels from upper elementary school through college.

Clear Entry Key: This is the key that clears the last entered value instead of clearing the entire operation. It is useful for the student who wants to learn to use it in the midst of a problem when one wrong value has been entered and only that value needs to be changed, but it is certainly not essential to anyone. On the other hand, having it on the calculator doesn't really hurt since an unknowing student who uses it as if it were the ordinary clear key will not run into any trouble because of this. Therefore, we will give it a rating of 3 for all school levels. It's up to the individual whether or not to get it, and whether or not to learn to use it correctly.

Percent Key: This is never an essential key since the percent sign simply represents dividing by one hundred and so the knowing student can perform the equivalent of the operation of the percent key using simple division. On the other hand, in problems which involve the percent sign, it's useful to have it available to follow the format of the problem. The only place where this key is really not needed is elementary school, but its presence really doesn't hurt in any way. Our rating for this key will therefore be a 3 for lower and upper elementary school and a 2 for junior high, senior high, and college.

Memory Keys: Memory capability is very useful, although not essential, from senior high school on up and the needs and capabilities of the individual student determine whether it is useful or not at the junior high school level since it does require a bit of practice. At the elementary school level it's not needed at all but it comes on many simple machines so it may not be possible to avoid it. All in all, it gets a rating of 3 for lower and upper elementary school, a rating of 3 also for junior high, and a rating of 2 for senior high and college.

Automatic Constant Key: This key is useful in repetitious addition, subtraction, multiplication, or division. It also turns out to be used in a large number of mathematical learning activities and games that have been developed for calculator application. For this reason it's useful at the elementary levels and also at higher levels, so we will give it a rating of 2 for every level, but for different reasons.

Exponentiation Key: This key is unnecessary at the elementary level so we will give it a rating of 4 there. At the junior high it can be used but can be done without just as well, so it gets a rating of 3. The key does begin to be quite useful from the senior high school level on up where individual exponentiation problems and problems involving exponentiation functions are encountered. At these levels we give it a rating of 2.

Logarithm Keys: Logarithm keys are almost essential if the calculator is to be used when this topic occurs at the high school level, and when logarithms and logarithm functions are used and studied at the college level. Of course it may be that logarithms will lose some of their importance in terms of pure computation as the curriculum changes in reaction to the computational capabilities of the calculator. But even then the topic will be important at the college level where logarithm functions are studied for their interesting properties rather than as computational aids. At the present time logarithms are used both at the high school and college levels so we give these keys a rating of 4 for lower and upper elementary school, 3 for junior high school, and 1 for senior high school and college.

Parentheses Keys: These keys are not really needed at the elementary level but are common on many basic machines so they may be hard to avoid. We will therefore give them a rating of 3 at the elementary levels, but if a good machine does not have them don't worry about it. At the junior and senior high school levels and in college the parentheses keys often allow the student to evaluate complicated mathematical expressions much more simply and quickly than if they are not available. Therefore, at these levels, we will give these keys a rating of 2.

Square Root Key: There is no real need for this key at the elementary level but it is on so many simple machines you may not be able to avoid it and so we will give it a rating of 3 rather than 4 at these levels. It becomes useful at the junior high level and is almost a necessity at the senior high and college levels for such topics as algebra, trigonometry, and probability and statistics. We therefore give it a rating of 2 for junior high school and 1 for senior high school and college.

Square and Reciprocal Keys: Neither of these keys is essential, but they can be quite handy to have in doing simple computations with one keystroke or in evaluating a mathematical expression with a short, compact keystroke sequence. We will give them a rating of 3 for the lower elementary school level because they are common keys on most calculators and hard to avoid. We will also give them a rating of 3 for the upper elementary school level, but this time because at this level the students have learned basic computation skills and can benefit from the opportunity to investigate these automatic computation keys and what they do to a given number. At the junior high school level they are useful to have but not essential so we will give them a rating of 2. Finally, once the student reaches senior high school it turns out that there are a variety of topics, including trigonometry, where these are very valuable keys to have and actually allow the student to evaluate important expressions that would have to be evaluated much less efficiently and quickly without them. For this reason I am going to give them a rating of 1 at the senior high school and college levels, although it would probably be more accurate to give a rating midway between essential and useful, perhaps a 1.5.

The ratings we've given to these features and special keys are presented below in chart form for ease of reference and use.

Keep in mind, however, that these are subjective ratings based on my own experiences and conversations with others, and that you should feel free to change any ratings that you feel do not accurately reflect your own child's capabilities and needs. Also keep in mind that the guiding principle in selecting a calculator is to get one with what you need but as simple as possible and then get a more sophisticated one when and only when that becomes necessary. Use the chart to determine which features and keys you want to get, and then ask the salesperson at the store you visit what they have with these features and keys. If they don't have what you want, don't simply settle for what's available, go to another store. The time spent in finding the appropriate calculator for your child's needs will be well worth it in terms of the short-term and long-term benefits he/she will derive from its use.

Calculator Selection Chart

(Ratings: 1 = Essential; 2 = Useful; 3 = Up to you; 4 = Avoid if Possible)

	Lower Elementary (K–3)	Upper Elementary (4–6)	Junior High (7–8, 9)	Senior High (9, 10–12)	College Level (Above 12)
Rechargeable	3	3	3	3	3
Adapter	3	3	2	2	2
Auto Power-Off	2	2	2	3	3
Continuous Memory	4	4	3	3	2
Hierarchy Logic	2	2	3	3	3
Clear "Error" Message	1	1	1	1	1
Scientific Display Capability and Keys	4	4	3	1	1
Shift Feature	4	4	3	3	3
Trigonometry Keys, with Degree and Radian Capability	4	4	2	1	1
Programmability	4	4	3	3	2
Fraction Capability	4	4	3	3	2
Solar Cell Power	3	3	3	3	3
Printing Capability	4	4	4	4	3
Plus/Minus or Change Sign Key	2	1	1	1	1
Clear Entry Key	3	3	3	3	3
Percent Key	3	3	2	2	2
Memory Keys	3	3	3	2	2
Automatic Constant	2	2	2	2	2
Exponentiation Key	4	4	3	2	2
Logarithm Keys	4	4	3	1	1
Parentheses Keys	3	3	2	2	2
Square Root Key	3	3	2	1	1
Square and Reciprocal Keys	3	3	2	1	1

6

The Calculator in the Home for the School-Age Child

In Chapter 1 we mentioned that even if calculators were nothing more than useful computational tools, it would still be extremely important for students to learn to use these tools correctly and efficiently or be at a distinct disadvantage when competing against those who had, both in school and after schooling is completed. Of course calculators are not just computational tools, although this is their most direct and obvious application. As we have seen in Chapter 2 they can be used, and are being used, in the schools in a variety of ways to motivate and interest students, to let students test out conjectures and generalizations in large numbers of cases, and to develop students' understanding of mathematical concepts. Nevertheless, the fact remains that the effectiveness of calculator use for any of these purposes is very dependent on the student's ability to do basic calculator computation. The student who has learned to do calculator computation and no longer has to worry about, or get sidetracked by, this basic use of the calculator will get much more out of all the other learning uses of the calculator than the student who gets bogged down in simple calculator arithmetic and spends an inordinate amount of time in doing and worrying about these basic calculations.

How does a student become competent with, and comfortable in, the use of the calculator? Certainly not by just using it in the classroom or when it is explicitly required in homework assignments and then putting it aside. The best and most effective way is by having a calculator available and using it in all the daily outside-of-school activities that require arithmetic computation as well as in schoolwork. After all, one of the major reasons why calculators have been accepted into the schools in spite of early resistance to them on the part of many educators was that they are available and useful (in fact, pervasive) in everyday life, and students should be taught to take advantage of their availability in ordinary daily activities. A simple analogy is in teaching a child to read and write, the other two "r's" in "reading, 'riting, and 'rithmetic." If you want your children to learn to read and write well you do not just assume that they will get all the practice they need to do this in the schools. You make it a point, in addition to what they learn and the practice they get in school, to read with them at home, to take them to the local library to get reading practice and to develop interest in reading, and you ask them to write "thank you" notes when they receive a birthday present or when they have visited a friend or a relative. This practice in the skills of reading and writing as an ordinary part of daily life complements and enhances what they are learning in school about these skills and is an essential ingredient in their acquisition. The same is true of calculator use. Children need to be shown that the calculator can be used to great advantage in a variety of everyday situations, and given practice in actually doing the computations in these situations. These experiences will not only help the child learn to accept and use the calculator as an ordinary part of daily life, it will also make him/her better prepared for all the uses to which the calculator can be put in his/her school.

In this chapter we will look at and discuss several "everyday" situations and activities in which the calculator can naturally be employed. It is not intended either that you must make use of the calculator in all these situations or that these are the only everyday situations in which the calculator can naturally be employed. They are presented merely as typical examples of situations in which using the calculator will seem normal and reasonable to your child rather than forced. Furthermore, we are not suggesting that every activity described here is appropriate for every school-age child. Each calculator use requires a certain level of mathematical development so don't try to involve a child in an activity that he/she is not ready for. However, since the mathematics involved in each use of the calculator is clearly and explicitly described, you should not find it too difficult to pick out the ones that are appropriate for your child's school level and mathematical knowledge.

It is our hope that with these situations as examples you will be able to find other activities you and your family partake in where you can begin to make use of the calculator as well. There are two points that must be made, however, in relation to these activities. First, while a side benefit of the activities discussed in this chapter may be to alert *you* to the many ways in which the calculator can profitably be employed in everyday life, the main target of these activities is your child. For this reason it is important that, as much as possible, your child participate in these activities and be the one who actually does the calculator computations. Of course you can oversee and check the computations, or the two of you can do them together, but watching someone else do the work is simply not the same as doing it yourself so try to have your child do the majority of the actual calculator work himself/herself with your help and guidance when necessary. Second, if the calculator is to be made use of in appropriate everyday situations in as normal and natural a way as a flashlight or a screwdriver is, then it must be made as easily available as a flashlight or a screwdriver. This means that you should not try to employ your $100 calculator in these activities any more than you would want to employ an antique Tiffany lamp as a flashlight. This would only inhibit the use of the calculator for ordinary situations, exactly the opposite of what we want to do. Instead, you should purchase one or two simple but sturdy $10 or $15 calculators. Keep one in your car's glove compartment for use on vacations or shopping trips or when you go out to eat, and keep the other in a desk drawer or kitchen drawer at home so that it is easily and immediately available whenever it might be needed. This will make you and your child feel as comfortable with getting and using the calculator whenever it is needed as you do getting a flashlight or screwdriver when it is needed, and this is exactly how the calculator should be viewed. Easy availability of a tool does not mean it can be misused or not taken care of; but it does mean it is a useful tool that you can and should get when appropriate and when needed. Now let's take a look at some of the activities and situations in which your child can use, and should be encouraged to use, his/her calculator.

TAKING A TRIP

A family trip provides a wealth of opportunities for using a calculator, both in the planning of the trip before you actually leave and in the keeping of records during the trip itself. If you make it a point to involve your child in the planning stage and in deciding what kinds of records to keep and why, then he/she can be given the job of keeping these records and doing the necessary calculator computations while you oversee these activities and make suggestions when appropriate.

Suppose, for example, that your family is planning a trip between New York City and Miami Beach, Florida. From the mileage charts given in most road atlases and on most highway maps for distances between major cities, it is easy to discover that the trip will be approximately 1500 miles each way if you take a fairly direct route. You can now use your calculator with the mathematical relationship between time, rate of speed, and distance to determine approximately how long the one-way trip will take you. The mathematical equation is:

$$\text{Distance} = \text{Rate} \times \text{Time}$$

or, equivalently,

$$\text{Time} = \text{Distance}/\text{Rate}.$$

Assuming you will travel at an average speed of approximately 55 miles per hour, your calculator used with this equation gives

$$\text{Time} = 1500 \text{ miles}/55 \text{ miles per hour}$$

$$= 27.27 \text{ hours},$$

or slightly more than 27 hours of driving one way. (Keep in mind that when we say "you can use your calculator to determine" we really mean your child can, or at worst you with your child.) You can now take this part of the planning stage one step further by deciding that to make the trip more enjoyable and less of a "rush," you only want to drive between 4 and 6 hours a day. Using the calculator you can use these minimum and maximum numbers of hours of driving per day to estimate the minimum and maximum number of miles you will be covering. This is illustrated below.

$$\text{Distance} = \text{Rate} \times \text{Time}$$

$$\text{Maximum Daily Distance} = 55 \text{ miles per hour} \times 6 \text{ hours}$$
$$= 330 \text{ miles};$$

$$\text{Minimum Daily Distance} = 55 \text{ miles per hour} \times 4 \text{ hours}$$
$$= 220 \text{ miles}.$$

You will therefore be traveling between 220 miles and 330 miles each day, and you can now use your maps and travel guides to plan appropriate daily stopping places which will be between 220 and 330 miles apart.

Another use of the calculator is in estimating how many gallons of gasoline your car will use on the trip down from New York to Miami Beach, and how much money you should budget for this expense. The relevant mathematical relationship is

$$\text{Miles per Gallon of Gas} = \text{Distance}/\text{Gallons}$$

or, equivalently,

$$\text{Number of Gallons of Gas} = \text{Distance}/\text{Miles per Gallon}.$$

If you know that on major highways your car gets approximately 15 miles per gallon of gas, then you can use your calculator to discover that you will need approximately

$$\text{Number of Gallons} = 1500 \text{ miles}/15 \text{ miles per gallon}$$
$$= 100 \text{ gallons of gas}.$$

Therefore, assuming a cost of approximately $1.35 a gallon of gas for 100 gallons gives

$$\text{Cost of Gas} = 1.35 \text{ per gallon} \times 100 \text{ gallons}$$
$$= 135$$

or about $135 dollars going down to Miami Beach and the same amount for the return trip. You can also add in the cost of tolls if your maps give that kind of information, but at least you have some idea how much money you must plan on spending just on gasoline for the trip.

Suppose, however, that rather than going directly from New York to Miami Beach you prefer to go in a somewhat less direct route so that you can stop at interesting places along the way. In this case the mileage given in the charts for New York City to Miami Beach will not be applicable since that mileage is for direct travel. However, you can still use the charts to obtain the individual distances between successive stops, then use the calculator to add these individual distances and in that way obtain the total distance for the trip. If you must travel on parts of several different lesser roads to get to your destination, you may have a choice of different combinations of roads to take. Once again, you can add all the pieces together with the calculator to get the total distance for each route and determine which is the shortest. Finally, since part of your trip may be on major highways where you can average 55 miles per hour, while the other part may be on local roads where you can only average 25 or 30 miles per hour, you can use the calculator and the distance-time-rate formula to calculate the approximate time for each type of travel and add these times together for total time of travel.

Once you are on the trip itself, a good way to make use of the calculator is in keeping records of such data as distance travelled each day, mileage per gallon of gas, and different types of expenses. The simplest way to do this is with a small notebook. Put the categories of expenses and the budget you have planned ahead of time on the first page or two of the book and then use two or three pages for keeping records for each day of the trip. Every time you fill the car's tank with gas, keep a record of the distance traveled from the last fill-up, the number of gallons of gas the car takes, and how much you pay. Every time money is spent on items like food, souvenirs, or hotel and motel accommodations the amount that was spent and what it was spent on should be recorded.

At the end of the day this information can be tabulated and analyzed to make sure you are still on your budget or, where necessary, to make modifications or adjustments in the planned budget. For example, to determine miles per gallon of gas you can use the calculator to divide the distance traveled between fill-ups of gasoline by the number of gallons the car needed. This will show whether or not you are getting the kind of mileage anticipated before the trip and therefore whether or not you are keeping to your projected gasoline budget. It will also allow you to compare the mileage you are getting on major highways where you can travel at a high and consistent rate of speed with the mileage you are getting in slow, stop and go city and local road driving. If you are getting much better mileage on the major highways than on the local roads you may prefer to skip some of the more "scenic" local roads in order to save money on gasoline that can then be spent in other more desirable ways.

You can also use the calculator to determine if the daily sum of expenditures for such items as food, lodging, gifts, etc. are keeping within your allotted budgets for those items. For example, suppose you planned on $250 for food expenses for the family on a 10-day trip (an average of $250/10 = $25 per day), and at the end of 5 days your records show you have already spent a total of $175 for this purpose. Then a simple calculator computation shows you have only $250 − $175 = $75 left for the remaining 5 days of the trip, and this gives an average of only $75/5 = $15 per day. Of course you can simply modify the original budget and decide to use more money than planned for food if you want to, but at least you would now know this and could plan for it. Perhaps this would be the time you decide to leave local roads and make the entire return trip on major highways so that the money saved on gasoline could be used in paying for continued good eating on the return trip.

Another use of the calculator is in "translating" distances given on roadsigns in the metric units of kilometers to equivalent but more "understandable" distances in miles; and maximum and minimum speeds given on roadsigns in units of kilometers per hour into equivalent but more "understandable" speeds in miles per hour. It's very easy to make such conversions with the aid of a calculator and is good practice in the simple arithmetic operation of multiplication. The relationship between kilometers (km) and miles (m) is

1 kilometer = 0.62 miles.

Therefore, to convert a given number of kilometers to miles, just multiply the number of kilometers by 0.62 on your calculator. For example, 75 kilometers would be converted in the following way:

$$75 \text{ kilometers} = 75 \times 0.62 \text{ miles}$$

$$= 46.5 \text{ miles.}$$

Similarly, speeds given in kilometers per hour can be converted to equivalent speeds in miles per hour by multiplying by 0.62. For example, a maximum speed limit of 90 kilometers per hour converts to

$$90 \text{ kilometers per hour} = 90 \times 0.62 \text{ miles per hour}$$

$$= 55.8 \text{ miles per hour.}$$

If you are spending part or all of your vacation in a foreign country with a currency different from our own, an informative activity is to use the calculator to convert amounts of money in the foreign currency into their U.S. dollar equivalents to get a better idea of what things cost. Just as the conversion of metric distances and rates of speed into more familiar units of distance and rate gives good practice in calculator multiplication, conversion of foreign currency into U.S. dollar equivalent gives good practice in calculator division. To convert any amount of money in a foreign currency to U.S. dollars, simply find out at a bank what one U.S. dollar is equivalent to, and divide the foreign currency amount by this constant. For example, suppose you are traveling in Canada and the rate of exchange while you are on your trip is

$$1 \text{ U.S. dollar} = 1.10 \text{ Canadian dollars.}$$

Then the constant to be used in conversions is 1.10, and a motel bill of 250 Canadian dollars would be equivalent to a bill for

$$\text{U.S. dollars} = \text{Canadian dollars}/1.10$$

$$= 250/1.10$$

$$= 227.27.$$

In other words, the 250 Canadian dollars are equivalent to only about 227.27 in U.S. dollars at the given exchange rate.

These are just some of the ways in which the calculator can be employed in planning and keeping track of expenses on a family trip. If such uses are made a normal and accepted part of family trips rather than something special, they will not only give your child a better understanding of the many informative uses to which a calculator can be put and a lot of practice in calculator computation; they will also impress upon him/her the need to plan and keep track of expenses so as to know where and how money is being spent instead of just spending it and wondering where it all went.

SHOPPING

One of the most common activities people do, and do often, is to go shopping. Shopping can refer to the supermarket where you go once a week to stock up on all the major food supplies your family will need; or it can refer to quick trips to a local little food store where you go when you need a quick gallon of milk and a loaf of bread; or it can refer to a department store or hardware store where you go to buy non-food items. In shopping at any of these stores you should take your calculator and, assuming your child is accompanying you, he/she can do the calculator computations we will discuss that are essential parts of a shopping trip for anyone who wants to be an informed and cost-conscious consumer. Once these uses of the calculator become familiar and accepted as a routine part of good shopping, your child can be expected to continue to employ them even when he/she goes shopping without you. Of course, you might also want to continue to employ them when you go shopping without your child.

The most basic use of the calculator as a shopping aid is to keep a running total of the cost of the items selected. This allows you to constantly monitor how much you have spent, how well you are keeping to your allotted budget for that day's shopping, and whether or not you can afford a few special items not on your shopping list but which you suddenly decide you would like to have. It also gives you some idea of the total cost of all the items when you have finished shopping and are standing on line to pay, so that if the total on the cash register looks way out of line with your own estimate it may indicate the clerk made an error in ringing up your sale.

The best way to keep a running total of your purchases is with a calculator having continuous memory so that values in memory are not lost when the calculator is turned off; and with the automatic memory addition and memory subtraction keys $\boxed{M^+}$ and $\boxed{M^-}$ respectively. (The key $\boxed{SUM}$ which appears on certain calculators does the same thing as $\boxed{M+}$.) The $\boxed{M^+}$ key allows you to keep the running total in memory so a mistake in entering the cost of any item into display will not affect the sum if you catch the error before pressing $\boxed{M^+}$. The continuous memory feature allows you to turn the calculator off after entering an item's price and then turning it on again when you are ready to add on another item's price in order to save the calculator battery's energy without losing the earlier subtotal. Of course you could simply leave the calculator on throughout the entire shopping trip if you don't have continuous memory, but this tends to drain the battery's energy. A calculator with an automatic power-off or shut-off feature also serves the intended purpose if the value in display or memory is not lost when the power-off or shut-off takes place. If, after selecting an item and entering its price into the running total using the $\boxed{M^+}$ key, you decide to put the item back, all you have to do is enter the item's price into display again and press the automatic memory sub-traction key $\boxed{M^-}$. This will take that item's price off the running total just as if it had never been entered in the first place. Finally, while you are standing on line waiting for your items to be rung up, you can figure in any savings due to coupons by simply entering the amounts of the coupons one at a time and pressing the $\boxed{M^-}$ key each time. This is especially helpful in supermarkets where discount coupons are common, but other types of stores with non-food items also advertise discount coupons in newspapers and circulars so it's useful in these stores as well.

Another use of the calculator while shopping is in making comparisons of products that come in different size packages by computing a "unit price" for each package. For example, suppose you want to buy a bottle of Heinz ketchup and your supermarket offers a 44 oz. bottle for $1.79 and a 32 oz. bottle for $1.39. The calculator can be used to determine how much each bottle is costing you "per ounce" to determine which is a better buy. To do this, think of the price of each bottle as number of cents to eliminate decimal numbers of dollars, and then divide the price in cents by the number of ounces in the bottle. This would give

44 oz. bottle: price per ounce = price/ounces

$$= 179/44 = 4.07¢ \text{ per oz;}$$

32 oz. bottle: price per ounce = price/ounces

$$= 139/32 = 4.34¢ \text{ per oz.}$$

Since the 44 oz. bottle costs less per ounce than the 32 oz. bottle, it would seem to be a better buy.

Of course, you might think that this use of the calculator is eliminated if your supermarket gives you the unit price for an item in addition to its total cost for the package. This would be true if you always intended to pay the listed price for the package. But with prices increasing almost every week for most items many people now use discount coupons and the unit price given by the store reflects the listed price, not the price of the item when you use your coupon on it. For example, consider once again the situation in which you want to buy a bottle of ketchup and suppose the store offers four different sizes with the size, total price, and unit price per ounce as given below.

Prices for Different Size Bottles of Ketchup

Size	Price	Price per Ounce
44 oz.	$1.79	4.07¢
32 oz.	$1.39	4.34¢
24 oz.	$1.29	5.38¢
14 oz.	$0.77	5.50¢

It would appear from this information that the 44 oz. bottle is the best buy since it costs the least per ounce. Suppose, however, that you have a 35¢ coupon good only on the 24 oz. size of this ketchup. In this case the real cost of the 24 oz. bottle of ketchup to you is not the listed price of $1.29 but $1.29 − $0.35 = $0.94, and so the given unit price does not reflect the real amount you would be paying. You would now have to find the true unit cost using the price of 94¢ that you would be paying, and with the calculator this is easily found to be

$$\text{Price per ounce} = \text{price/ounces} = 94/24$$

$$= 3.92¢.$$

In other words, taking into account the coupon you have, the 24 oz. bottle of ketchup is really a better buy than all the other sizes, including the 44 oz. bottle. This is the kind of realistic unit price comparison that must be employed whenever you have a coupon for a product, and it is the calculator that allows you to make these unit price computations quickly and easily.

Another difficulty with the types of unit prices that are often provided is that they are not always in the units that give you the most informative and useful comparison. For example, suppose you are interested in buying a package of General Electric 75 watt lightbulbs. You notice a package of 2 "longlife white" GE lightbulbs with a price of $2.30, and a package of 4 "soft-white" GE lightbulbs with a price of $2.79. The unit price information given is price per lightbulb for each package with all the information provided as shown below.

Comparison of Light Bulb Prices

	Number of Bulbs in Package	Cost of Package	Unit Cost per Bulb
Long Life	2	$2.30	$1.15
Soft-White	4	$2.79	$0.70

Based on this information, it would seem that the soft-white bulbs are a much better buy since they cost much less per bulb than the long life bulbs. However, cost per bulb may not be the best unit for comparing the two types of bulb. If you look closely at each package you will notice that the package itself gives information on how many hours of life you can expect, on the average, from each type of bulb. Since the usefulness of a bulb depends very much on how long it will continue to work, perhaps a more appropriate unit of comparison would be unit cost per hour of use rather than unit cost per bulb. For example, the package of 2 long life lightbulbs indicates that each bulb will give approximately 1500 hours of use so the package gives approximately 2 × 1500 = 3000 hours of use. Similarly, the package of 4 soft-white lightbulbs indicates that each bulb will give approximately 750 hours of use so the package gives approximately 4 × 750 = 3000 hours of use. If we now use our calculator to divide cost per package by number of hours of use per package we obtain the cost per hour of use as shown below.

	Hours of Use in Package	Cost of Package	Unit Cost per Hour of Use
Long Life	3000	$2.30	230/3000 = .077¢
Soft-White	3000	$2.79	279/3000 = .093¢

Using this more appropriate unit of measurement for purposes of comparison, it's clear from the unit cost per hour of use that the long life lightbulbs are the better buy. This is because, while the long life lightbulbs cost more than the soft-white per bulb, each bulb lasts twice as long. Notice that while this is the kind of unit cost comparison you might like to make, you must do the actual computations yourself since this is not the kind of information the store's unit price information provides. And it is the calculator that allows you to do these computations and obtain these desired unit prices.

EATING OUT

If your family is like most American families, the increased costs of eating out at regular sit-down, table service restaurants have forced you to shift much of your eating out to fast food-type establishments like McDonald's, Burger King, Kentucky Fried Chicken, Arthur Treacher's Fish and Chips, or Pizza Hut.

Whether you eat at these establishments or buy your food there and take it home to eat, the calculator can be used to help you make sure you are getting your money's worth, to help you plan what you will buy there, and to help you stay on your food budget if you have decided that such a budget is necessary. Since children generally love fast food restaurants it is also natural for them to be involved in going to such restaurants and planning what to buy, and this can be made to involve calculator computation as we will now see.

The first thing to do is to get a menu with available items and prices from any fast food establishment you tend to go to, and keep it at home for purposes of planning. Some restaurants actually have paper take-home menus, especially those which allow phone-in orders. For example, my local Pizza Hut restaurant gave me a pocket sized menu, but I had to write in the prices myself from the regular menu in the restaurant. At other restaurants you may have to make up your own list of items and prices when you are there one time. The menu below was written down one day recently while my family had breakfast Sunday morning at McDonald's.

Sample McDonald's Menu with Items and Prices

Big Mac	$1.40	Fries	55¢/70¢
Quarter Pounder	$1.30	milk	40¢
Fish Sandwich	$0.95	Coke	50¢/55¢/65¢
Chicken McNuggets	$1.35	shake	75¢
Hamburger	$0.55	sundae	59¢
Cheeseburger	$0.68	tea, coffee	35¢

Before taking the family to McDonald's, for example, you could now use a calculator with this price list to estimate how much the entire meal will cost. You can even do this in the car on the way to the restaurant if you keep a price list and a calculator in the glove compartment. A Big Mac and Coke for $1.40 + .50 = $1.90 does not sound like much, but when everyone wants that plus french fries and dessert the total cost can add up to a considerable amount. Planning the family purchase and how much it will cost beforehand is a good habit to get into since children's stomachs can sometimes overwhelm their reason when they get to the restaurant. Another possibility is to put each person on a certain budget allowance so that they can choose whatever they want as long as they stay within their budget. The calculator can then be used to sum the prices for desired items to make sure the meal does not go over the given limit. For example, your child may at first decide to have a Big Mac, large french fries, a strawberry shake and a chocolate sundae for dessert. However, if his/her budget limitation is $3.00, a quick summing of the prices of these items with the calculator shows they will cost $3.44 and this is over the limit. One possible solution is to give up the chocolate sundae which, the calculator shows, will reduce the total cost to an acceptable $3.44 − $0.59 = $2.85; or to keep the sundae and get a Quarter Pounder instead of a Big Mac, a small order of french fries instead of a large order, and a small Coke instead of a strawberry shake. This would give a total cost of $1.30 + $0.55 + $0.50 + $0.59 = $2.94, again an acceptable level.

Very often a restaurant will have a "special" which gives a combination of items that is supposedly a much better buy than if you were to order each of the items individually. The calculator can be used to add together the cost of all the individual items to determine whether or not the special really is as good an offer as it is supposed to be. For example, my local Arthur Treacher's Fish and Chips offers, in addition to other items and specials, the items listed below with their individual prices, and the accompanying special with its price.

Some Arthur Treacher Items and Specials

Special

Original Fish Platter: 2 fish fillets, chips, 2 hush puppies, cole slaw	$2.59

Individual Items

cole slaw 44¢	chips 69¢
1 fish fillet 99¢	3 hush puppies 39¢

Using the calculator to add together the prices of the individual items that comprise the Original Fish Platter special (and ignoring the fact that the special gives only 2 hush puppies while the individual order gives 3), we obtain a total price of

$$2 \times .99 + .69 + .39 + .44$$
$$= 1.98 + .69 + .39 + .44$$
$$= 3.50.$$

Therefore, the special which costs only $2.59 gives a savings of $3.50 − $2.59 = $0.91 or 91¢, assuming that you actually want everything in the special. This would seem to be a good "special."

On the other hand, consider the coffee shop that offers the following "breakfast special" and individual items to its customers.

Breakfast Special

---

2 eggs (any style), potatoes, toast, small glass of juice, coffee or tea—$1.49

Individual Items

---

2 eggs with potatoes—75¢   toast—20¢
coffee or tea—35¢   small juice—50¢

If you use your calculator to add up the individual item prices you do find that they sum to .75 + .20 + .35 + .50 = 1.80 so your savings with the special is $1.80 − $1.49 = $0.31 = 31¢. However, if you do not really want juice with your meal, the sum of all the other items only adds up to .75 + .20 + .35 = 1.30. In other words, you can think of the breakfast special as giving all the non-juice items at their individual prices and the juice, ordinarily a 50¢ item, for only an additional 19¢. However, if you don't really want the juice you can save yourself this additional 19¢ by buying all the other items individually and paying only $1.30.

If you do go to a regular, non-fast food restaurant, the calculator can still be usefully employed. For example, your child can be given the very important job (with you checking the arithmetic, of course) of using the calculator to add together all the individual prices on the check to make sure the sum is correct. The percent key can then be used to verify the tax listed on the bill and, if everything is correct, used to determine the size of the tip you want to leave. Waiters and waitresses are often quite busy and a mistake in addition or in tax is not as unusual an occurrence as we would like to think. This normal verification of the check is a good habit to develop at an early age, and the availability of the calculator makes it a simple matter rather than a real chore.

One final use of the calculator in eating out, or bringing prepared food into the house to eat, should be mentioned. You often have a choice of sizes of items to buy, such as when you must choose between a small or a large pizza. It's informative to use the calculator to determine which size is the better buy and this is fairly easy to do. For example, suppose you do in fact want to buy and bring back to the house a pizza for your family of four to eat. Your local pizza parlor or pizza restaurant offers a choice of a small pizza (12 inches in diameter) for $3.40 or a large pizza (18 inches in diameter) for $6.20, with the small pizza supposedly serving 1 or 2 people and the large pizza supposedly serving 3 or 4 people. At first glance you might want to buy the large pizza since it serves 4 people and you have 4 people in your family. On the other hand, the large pizza costs approximately twice what the small pizza costs and is only 1-1/2 the diameter of the small pizza. Perhaps you would do better buying two small pizzas for 2 × $3.40 = $6.80 instead of one large pizza for $6.20 and not only have enough pizza for your family that night but a few pieces left over to reheat for lunch the next day. Apparently, a comparison of 1 large pizza to 2 small pizzas in terms of unit cost is in order, and with the calculator it is fairly easy to do. Since both small and large pizzas are approximately the same thickness, the amount of pizza you get in each case really depends on the area of the pies. And, as any high school student can tell you, the area of a circle with radius r is given by the formula

area of circle = Pi × r^2 = 3.14 × r^2, approximately.

Since the radius of a circle is half its diameter, we find the following areas for a small and large pizza, respectively, with the aid of a calculator:

$$\text{small pizza area} = 3.14 \times r^2 = 3.14 \times 6^2$$
$$= 3.14 \times 36 = 113.04 \text{ sq. inches;}$$
$$\text{large pizza area} = 3.14 \times r^2 = 3.14 \times 9^2$$
$$= 3.14 \times 81 = 254.34 \text{ sq. inches.}$$

It is now easy to see that in terms of area, two small pizzas give 2 times 113.04 or only 226.08 sq. inches while one large pizza gives 254.34 sq. inches. Therefore, while two small pizzas cost 60 cents more than one large pizza, they give 28.26 sq. inches less area than one large pizza. Based on these comparisons, the large pizza is a much better buy than two small pizzas.

IN THE NEIGHBORHOOD

If your child belongs to an organization like the Boy Scouts, the Girl Scouts, or even his/her high school marching band or French Club, he/she may be involved in raising money for these organizations by selling some product to your neighbors. Whenever something is being sold and amounts of money must be collected or simply kept track of, the calculator can be used for the accompanying arithmetic computations. For example, suppose your daughter is a Girl Scout and is going around the neighborhood selling Girl Scout Cookies. She most likely would be given an order sheet like the one illustrated below on which she would keep a record of what types of cookies were ordered, how many boxes of each, and the total amount of money to be collected for that order.

Girl Scout Cookies Order Sheet

Customer Name	Mint Chips ($1.50 @)	Chocolate Fudge ($2.00 @)	Vanilla Creme ($1.75 @)	Total Cost of Order
Jennifer P.		2		$4.00
Nicole P.		1	1	$3.75
Sam P.		2	2	$7.50
Paul L.	3			$4.50
Jenny L.	1	1	1	$5.25
Arielle G.	2	1		$5.00

On this sheet your daughter would enter the number of boxes of each type of cookie ordered, and then the cost of the order. However, since different types of cookies usually cost different amounts, this means she must multiply the cost of each type by its corresponding number of boxes, and then add up all these individual subtotals for the total cost of the order. If she is collecting at the time she takes the order she may also have to give change when the customer does not have the exact amount readily available. All of these arithmetic computations are easier to do, and are less prone to being done incorrectly, if they are done with a simple four function calculator (i.e. a calculator that can do addition, subtraction, multiplication, and division). Of course this also gives a lot of very helpful practice in simple calculator arithmetic.

The same type of computations are involved for any other type of group fund-raising activity, such as when members of the high school marching band sell cases of Florida grapefruit and oranges to raise money for a spring vacation trip to Miami Beach.

If your son or daughter delivers newspapers, once every week or two they must collect for the deliveries from the people along their route. Once again a calculator can be used to determine how much each person must pay (people who only have weekday papers delivered obviously do not pay as much per week or per month as those who have weekday papers plus the Sunday paper delivered) and how much change must be given if the exact amount is not available.

Many high school students have part time jobs, or weekend jobs, or jobs during their vacation periods in which they get paid a certain rate per hour, perhaps with an extra amount per hour when they work overtime or on extra weekends. They should be encouraged to keep a record of how many hours they work and how many overtime hours they work so they can use a calculator to determine how much pay they can expect to receive in their paychecks. One of the consequences of keeping such records is they can catch an error in their pay if an error occurs. Another consequence is that they will come to realize that they do not get the entire amount they are supposedly being paid for the job. Instead, some of it goes automatically to federal, state, and possibly local taxes, and some may even go to Social Security. While this may be somewhat disheartening to the youngster who thought that a job paying $3 per hour would actually give him/her $3 take home pay for each hour worked, it does provide a realistic picture of what he/she can expect and must plan to live on when he/she gets a full-time and permanent job in the future. Besides, the youngster who knows that exactly 25% of his/her paycheck should be taken out for taxes will be very careful in using the calculator to verify that it is in fact 25% and not more whenever a paycheck is received.

SPORTING EVENTS

If your son or daughter is a diehard sports fan, or even just likes to keep track of a particular team and go to a game now and then, you can use the calculator with him or her both in planning before the season opens and during the season as well.

For example, suppose your child just loves the baseball Detroit Tigers and enjoys going to their games. Before the season begins you obtain a price list for individual game tickets and for season tickets, and you discover that for the first baseline box seats you'd like to have the cost is $8 for one game but only $320 for all 80 home games during the season. Since a season ticket assures you of those desirable seats every time you go to a game, the question you might want to answer is how many games you'd need to attend during the season for it to be worth buying the season ticket. To answer this question, all you have to do is use your calculator to divide the price of a season ticket by the price of a single game ticket. The result will be the number of games you'd need to attend for the season ticket to pay itself off. Given the prices suggested here, the division would yield 320/8 = 40. In other words, if you attend exactly 40 of the 80 games during the season, your season ticket will not have cost any more than if you had paid for those games on an individual basis and at the same time you've been able to guarantee yourself the particular seats you wanted. If you attend even more than 40 games you get the seats you want and save money over the individual price as well.

Youngsters often have a favorite team and favorite players. If you take your child to a baseball game, or even if you're just watching the game on television, you can use the calculator to play a game within the game you're watching. Have your child select two or three of his/her favorite players in the game to be his/her "team"; then you do the same, but making sure none of your players are on your child's team. The winner of this calculator "game" is the person whose "team" has a higher team "batting average" at the end of the baseball game. Batting average is the number of hits divided by the total number of times at bat with walks being ignored. Playing this game requires keeping a list of the opposing team members, keeping track of the number of hits each team gets and the number of "at-bats," and dividing hits by at-bats to obtain a team batting average. Since a large part of the enjoyment of such a game is seeing who is ahead all through the game a "running batting average" should be computed for each team with the aid of the calculator at the end of every inning or two. Any of your child's friends who happen to be around can also be given "teams" and allowed to play the game.

While the game just described involves and provides practice in calculator division, an alternate version of it can be used to give practice in addition as well, and possibly even multiplication. In this alternate version of the game everyone still chooses a three-player team and keeps a record of how many times players come to bat and how well they do, but what is compared is a "power average" rather than a simple "batting average." While a batting average essentially gives a batter a 1 whenever the batter gets a hit, a 0 whenever the batter makes an out, and averages these 1's and 0's, the power average gives different numbers of points for different types of hits. For example, while an out still gets 0 points, a single gets 1 point; a double gets 2 points; a triple gets 3 points; and a home run gets 4 points. To obtain the team's power average at any time just add up the points of the team for all different types of hits, divide by the number of times at bat, and the result is the power average. (Keep in mind that a power average can be greater than 1, as opposed to a regular batting average which can never be greater than 1. So if you or your child gets a result greater than 1 it does not automatically mean an error was made in the computation.)

To simplify the computation of team power averages at the

end of each inning or two, keep a chart like the one illustrated below.

Team A Power Scoreboard

(Power Average = Total Points/At Bats)

Type of Result	Points	Number	Points × Number = Point Total
Out	0		
Single	1		
Double	2		
Triple	3		
Home Run	4		
		At Bats =	Total Points =

This table can be kept up to the minute by filling it in with a pencil and changing the numbers in the last two columns each time a player gets a hit or makes an out. Notice that when the calculator is used to add up the "Number" column the result is "At Bats"; when the values in the "Point" column are multiplied by the values in the "Number" column the results are the points for that type of result; and when the calculator is used to add up the final column the result is "Total Points." The power average is then obtained by dividing Total Points by At Bats.

These are just some of the ways in which the calculator can be used in and about sporting events. With a little imagination you can probably develop your own uses in addition to, or instead of, these, and in other sports than baseball as well.

IN THE HOME

As we suggested in the beginning of this chapter, the calculator should be made available and easily accessible in the home so that it can be naturally made use of whenever its use as a computational tool arises. In this section we'd like to mention just a few of these natural and obvious uses. You can probably add to the list from your own experiences and at-home activities.

A simple but obvious use of the calculator is with cooking activities. When the child is cooking or helping a parent to cook, the calculator can be used in many necessary ways. Suppose, for example, that you are planning on surprising the family with pancakes for breakfast. The recipe on the back of the box indicates that for approximately 12 pancakes you should use 2 cups of mix; 2 eggs; 1 cup of milk; and 3/4 tablespoon of butter. Your family, however, is rather large with three children and a pair of hungry parents, and from past experience you know they will need about 30 pancakes. To modify the given amount of each ingredient for this number of pancakes simply divide the number you want by the number the recipe gives and multiply each amount by that value. In our illustration this constant multiplier would be 30/12 which gives 2.5 using the calculator. Then, again using the calculator, the correct amounts of each ingredient would be: 2.5 × 2 = 5 cups of mix; 2.5 × 2 = 5 eggs; 2.5 × 1 = 2.5 cups of milk; and 2.5 × (3/4) = 1.875 or 1-7/8 tablespoons of butter. The calculator can be used to modify the given amounts of ingredients in any recipe when you want more or less of the result than the recipe provides.

A second use of the calculator in cooking is in baking time. Suppose you are going to cook a stuffed turkey for Thanksgiving. The cooking instructions in your cookbook indicate 20 minutes of cooking for each pound of a large turkey, and yours is a large turkey of 15 pounds. Your child can now use the calculator to multiply the time per pound by number of pounds to obtain 20 × 15 = 300 minutes of cooking time. To make this amount of time more understandable your child can now use the calculator to divide the number of minutes by 60 to convert the time into hours. This gives 300/60 = 5 hours of cooking time.

The calculator can also be used to verify bills you receive routinely. For example, when you receive your monthly telephone bill it most likely contains individual amounts for monthly service, for long-distance calls, for special services, and for tax. Your child can now help you verify the total before paying by using the calculator to add up all these values. Similarly, when you receive your bill for electric use, it will generally tell how many kilowatt-hours of electricity were used, the charge per kilowatt hour, the previous meter reading and the present meter reading.

Your child can now use the calculator to subtract the previous meter reading from the present reading and verify number of kilowatt hours used; multiply this amount by the charge per kilowatt hour to verify the charge; multiply this by the listed percent for tax to verify the charge for tax; and add up all these values to check the total bill. Similar uses of the calculator are easily developed for other standard bills you receive as well, with your child doing the major portion of the calculator work and you available to help out and check the computations when asked.

One final at-home use of the calculator we will mention is in computing the amount of paint or wallpaper that would be needed if you are planning to paint or wallpaper one or more rooms. This computation requires multiplying the height by the length of all walls, and the length by the width of the ceiling if you are painting the room and the ceiling is to be painted as well as the walls. Then the surface area of each window must be computed and subtracted from the total since windows are usually not painted or wallpapered, and the door areas subtracted off if they too are not to be covered. All of this involves numerous multiplications, additions and subtractions, and they are readily and correctly carried out with the aid of a calculator. Furthermore, if you've already involved your child in planning and evaluating the amount of paint or wallpaper that will be needed for the job, it's easier to keep them involved when the actual job of painting or wallpapering begins than if you did all the planning and suddenly demand their involvement only when the actual work begins.

7

The Calculator in the Home for the Pre-School Child

If you've ever watched a pre-schooler at play, you have some idea of their incredible and inexhaustible natural curiosity. They are intrigued by colors, sounds, and movement, and even the most ordinary of objects (ordinary to the normal grown up, that is) can serve the pre-schooler as a source of exciting exploration and play. Since calculators exhibit just these characteristics that children find so fascinating (the colors of the different keys; the sounds that accompany the pressing of the keys on the so-called "musical" calculators or even the ordinary clicking sound when a key on a non-musical calculator is pressed; and the movement on the display screen as keys are pressed and displayed values appear, change, and disappear), it's no wonder that parents who leave a calculator lying around within reach of a pre-schooler often find the child playing with it as if it were one of their own toys. This natural attraction of pre-schoolers for calculators as toys to play with and learn about offers the parent a wonderful opportunity for giving the pre-schooler a head start in becoming familiar and comfortable with these machines before they actually have to come face to face with them in a formal classroom setting.

There are two main reasons for allowing, and even encouraging, pre-schoolers to play with calculators. The first reason has to do with the actual operation of the calculator rather than any particular learning benefits, although it is true that children at this stage of development "learn" in a general sense from all their experiences and actions. There are certain operating procedures that any calculator user must learn at some stage of their exposure to these machines if they are ever to make use of them in a correct and effective manner. Some of the more basic of these operating procedures are: (i) turning the calculator on and off; (ii) the use and location of the clear key; (iii) recognition of "unusual" calculator displays that indicate special occurrences like an error message or a message that a value has been put into a memory location; (iv) looking at the display after a number key has been pressed to verify that the number that appears is in fact the number you wanted to appear; and (v) learning the order in which keys need to be pressed, and exactly which keys need to be pressed, to perform simple arithmetic operations like addition of two one-digit numbers. While these basics are easy for an adult to understand and remember once they have been explained and demonstrated, they can be a major obstacle to an elementary student who is, at the same time, trying to cope with the major upheaval of being separated from his/her parents and being put into a new and very unusual school environment. Even if the child does not confront the calculator in the formal school setting until junior or senior high school (although, as we saw in Chapter 2, the calculator is increasingly being used at and recommended for use at the elementary level), learning its operating procedures is still a major task because it must then be accomplished at the same time the child is having to learn the mathematics the calculator will be used on. By introducing the pre-schooler to the calculator in the guise of an interesting and non-threatening toy, with all the attractions of color and sound and movement that he/she enjoys and is used to in his/her other toys, the child can become familiar with many of the more basic of these operating features over a period of months and even years instead of having to learn them in a matter of days or at most weeks when they are suddenly encountered in the classroom. This is also an excellent way to teach the child good habits in the care of the calculator. The child of four or five who learns to turn off the calculator and put it carefully away when he/she is finished playing with it the same way all his/her other toys must be carefully put away at the end of each day's play time will continue with these good habits when they once again encounter the calculator as a learning tool years later instead of accidentally leaving it on overnight and wearing its battery down or even damaging it by careless or sloppy handling.

The second reason for introducing the pre-schooler to the calculator has to do with the calculator's usefulness in giving the child better preparation for the mathematics he/she will be exposed to when they later enter formal schooling. There is no question that the child who has been supplied with appropriate experiences and directed activities is more ready to learn, and more capable of learning, when he/she later enters school. This is one of the reasons why educational television for pre-schoolers such as *Sesame Street* has been so successful and long-running and why many parents nowadays send their pre-schoolers to nursery school. While these activities serve as wonderful "baby-sitters" and social experiences, they also ready the child for the learning experiences they will encounter in elementary school. To give just one example of this, consider the pre-schooler who has learned how to count from one to ten in order before entering school. This child will be better prepared to answer the teacher's question "What comes after five?" in kindergarten or first grade than the child who must first learn to count to ten in the classroom before understanding what this question is asking and being able to answer it. When we realize that asking "What comes after five?" is the precursor to the arithmetic question "What is 5 plus 1?" we can see learning to count from one to ten in the home as a means of "preparing" or "readying" the child for what will be encountered in the school. With regard to the importance of giving the pre-schooler the kinds of experiences that will help prepare them for when they enter school, it might be of interest to quote a statement from the book *Mathematics Begins* (John Wiley & Sons, 1970). This book developed out of the Nuffield Mathematics Project in England, which was established by the Nuffield Foundation in 1964 for the purpose of studying and improving the traditional elementary mathematics curriculum. In it, the statement is made that

> The background of experience of the child determines the starting point when he comes to school. If he has not been fortunate enough to have enjoyed a rich and varied set of activities in these early years—if he has not been able to discuss these with some-

one who uses language with flexibility and imagination, then these opportunities must be made available in school as a first priority, for on such a foundation does his future development depend.

The purpose of this chapter is to show you how to use the calculator to provide your pre-schooler with the "rich and varied set of activities in these early years" that are referred to in this quote, at least in the area of mathematics. To do this, we will describe and discuss a number of activities that involve the calculator and that are appropriate for the pre-schooler. The first set of activities will explicitly concentrate on letting the child become familiar with some of the calculator's more basic operating procedures rather than on any specific mathematical learning or "pre-learning." For these activities we will discuss when these activities might be appropriate; how to guide the child through them and the type of language to use; and the purpose of the activities. The second set of activities will be "readiness" or "preparation" activities and experiences for specific later learning tasks in mathematics. For each of these activities we will discuss the stage of development at which they might be appropriate; how to lead the child to, and guide him/her through, the activity; and the specific later mathematical learning task the activity is preparing the child for and how the activity fits the learning task.

Before getting to the actual calculator activities and experiences, some general comments are in order. First, while "readying" and "preparation" is possible and useful for all children, there is no one correct or appropriate time when such activities and experiences can be said to be "right" for your particular child. This is clear from one of the most enlightened theories of children's development in understanding and thinking of the twentieth century, the theory of cognitive development by the Swiss psychologist Jean Piaget. In this theory Piaget asserts that while the four major stages of a child's development are fixed in order, the time at which any particular child passes from one stage to the next is determined by both internal factors such as the child's normal maturation, and external factors such as the experiences the child has had and the activities he/she has participated in. Therefore, although we can try to help with the external factors of experience and activity, we cannot and should not force the child before he/she is internally ready for this advancement. Luckily, we don't have to try and guess when the child will be ready for the activities described here, we simply have to be open to and aware of what his/her actions tell us. If you try one of the activities or ask some of the suggested questions and the child does not evidence any interest in what you are suggesting, then he/she simply is not ready and should not be forced. It may be that the next week when you try the same opening he/she will be ready and the interest will be there, or it may be that you'll have to wait a few months before he/she is ready and mature enough to understand and become involved. Simply try different approaches periodically and when the child is ready he/she will respond. Furthermore, don't be upset or discouraged if he/she seems to be slower to enter into or do well in some of the activities described here than you think he/she should be or than you think other children are. There is no timetable that all children follow, and a lack of interest or development in one particular area is usually due to a special interest or development in some other equally important area. For example, the child who learns to talk late may simply be too involved in active and imaginative play to need or want to communicate verbally. Any pre-school preparation a child receives is better and more helpful than no preparation, but forcing your child into activities when he/she is not ready or not inclined to be so involved can have a negative effect on his/her later learning and even his/her later interest in learning. The clearest indication that the child is ready to be involved in any of the activities described here is their obvious and natural interest and excitement when the suggestion is made and the activity is employed. Simply use these ideas whenever time is available and the child seems receptive just the way you would read to (or with) your child periodically when he/she is receptive or help him/her to recognize and begin to spell the names of objects when he/she seems interested or asks for your help.

The other point has to do with the actual calculators that are used and their availability to the child. Obviously you don't want a pre-schooler to be using and quite possibly sometimes misusing your favorite and most expensive calculator as he/she learns about it and plays with it. A simple, inexpensive calculator will do just as well, and perhaps even better, since then you won't worry about leaving the calculator out all day or your child even wanting to take it to bed with him/her the way he/she might do with any other enjoyable and fascinating toy. In fact, it might be a good idea to have three or four different, simple and inexpensive calculators around the house that the child can periodically play with or even ask for. Different calculators have different attractions and this variety helps generate the interest and motivation that we want the child to develop. For example, I have several different calculators that my three-year-old son Timothy loves to play with for different reasons. There is my Casio musical calculator that he calls "the calculator that makes music"; my Sharp calculator that "makes funny numbers" (because it gives the error message "0.0.0.0.0.0.0.0" when he presses certain keys that create illegal operations); my Sears solar cell powered calculator that he likes to turn off by placing his hand over the solar cells and cutting off the light source; and my "big calculator in a case" that he likes to take out of and put into its case that zippers open and closed. He doesn't always have them all out, and in fact I will usually not let him have more than at most two to play with at any one time. But there are occasions when he wants to make music on a calculator, and there are times when he wants to press the keys and get the funny number to show up on the display for his mother and his grandmother, and this variety fuels his interest and gives him more and more varied calculator experiences than if he were restricted to only one special calculator. Let me hurry to point out, however, that none of these calculators is either very sophisticated or very expensive so that if they were accidentally damaged it would not be a catastrophe; and that I do gently demand that he treat them well and that he turn them off when he is finished playing with them. It is an interesting sidelight to all this playing with and access to calculators that Timothy is as excited as I am whenever I buy and bring home a new calculator to play with and investigate. In certain activities I will mention that a particular type of calculator is either required or better suited to the activity than other calculators. If you don't have such a calculator and don't want to buy one (for yourself, of course, with your child simply having access to it by asking you), then simply do the activity as best you can or skip it. Most of the activities do not require any special type of calculator and they will provide more than enough exposure and experiences for a good pre-school mathematics preparation.

One final remark before we introduce these calculator activities. The first seven activities relate to calculator operating procedures and are fairly simple and straightforward. They can generally be done with fairly young pre-schoolers, possibly as young as two and a half and three years of age, and do not have to be done in any particular order. The next seven, activities #8 through #14, are arranged in general in order of their levels of difficulty. Therefore, while the first few of these can be used with as young a child as three or so years of age, the last few would probably only be employed with a somewhat older pre-schooler and after the first three or four of these activities (#8 through # 11) have been comfortably mastered by the child. Keep in mind that you are not trying to teach the child the mathematics that is described in these pre-mathematical learning activities, you are just trying to prepare them for when these mathematical topics are encountered by them later on when they are actually in elementary school and in the classroom setting. Now it's time to get to the actual activities so take out your calculator or calculators and let's get started.

ACTIVITIES FOR CALCULATOR OPERATING PROCEDURES

Activity #1: Turning the Calculator On and Off

As simple as turning the calculator on and off seems, it's necessary to instill in the young child the habit of turning the calculator off when he/she is finished using it if he/she is to be expected to do this routinely when using the calculator in elementary school and beyond. To need the calculator for school work and turn it on only to find that it was accidentally left on overnight and its battery is dead can be as frustrating (and even traumatic) to a child as to try to start the family car and discover that its headlights were accidentally left on overnight and the car's battery is dead can be to an adult. This kind of frustration and impediment to classroom learning can be avoided if turning the calculator off is made an ordinary part of the child's being allowed to use it in the first place. Furthermore, quite aside from developing good habits, requiring the child to turn the calculator off and even to turn the calculator on for himself/herself can have unanticipated benefits of a quite different sort. Since there is very little uniformity in calculators, there is great variety in the location of commonly used keys and even how these keys are used on a calculator. For example, recall from Chapter 4 all the different types of error messages calculators have and the different symbols and operating procedures for clear keys on different calculators. It can be difficult for someone who is used to a particular arrangement and operation of calculator keys to adapt to other calculators with other arrangements and procedures when their own calculator fails or when a new one is bought. For example, I have had adults in my graduate level statistics and math courses who could not adapt to my calculator when their own malfunctioned during an examination because my calculator required them to use a shift key for certain necessary operations whereas theirs did not have shift keys. Incredibly, they preferred to finish the exam without a calculator at all rather than have to adapt to the different way my calculator operated. Since there are a variety of ways in which different calculators are turned on and off, by letting the young child encounter and deal with this variety in something as simple as turning the calculator on and off they will be better prepared to accept and deal with variety in operation of calculators in other ways when and if they need to later on. As an illustration, some calculators have a switch that turns the calculator on and off; some have one or two keys on the keyboard; some have more than one mode of being turned on such as the musical calculators which can be turned to an "on" position which produces musical notes when keys are pressed or to an "on" position that makes the calculator remain silent when keys are pressed; and some calculators, the solar cell calculators, are turned off by covering the solar cells with your hand or by being placed in the case, and either have a key to turn them on or automatically turn themselves on as soon as light hits the cells.

This activity simply consists of allowing, and in fact encouraging, the child to turn the calculator on himself/herself when he/she wants to use it and casually but consistently asking the child if he/she turned it off when the child is finished playing with it. Of course you wouldn't make these demands or ask these questions of a one-year-old, since a one-year-old does not really have either the required understanding or manual dexterity. But you could and should require this of any child who is three years or older since they can understand what you are asking them and why, and they do have the manual dexterity to do it, although they may sometimes need and ask for your help. A young child generally likes the power and feeling of being grown up that turning the calculator on and off by himself/herself gives, but they also often don't want to be grown up and independent so don't force the child to do it if he/she doesn't want to. The times they want to do it by themselves will increase as they get older and will provide them with all the practice and experience they need.

Activity #2: Clearing the Calculator Display

Teaching the pre-schooler to clear the calculator's display by pressing the appropriate key prepares the child for the later acceptance of specific keys to perform specific operations and tasks.

On most calculators the clear key is separated from the other keys by being placed somewhere at the top of the calculator keyboard, and it is usually given a special color to make it easier for the user to find it. You should try to use a calculator that not only has the clear key separated from all the other keys and colored, but of a color different from any of the other keys as well. This allows you to say to the child "press the red key" or "press the gold key," whatever the clear key's color happens to be, rather than the more general and less obvious "press the clear key." In fact, if you can refer to this key by color, then you can even use this activity with a child as young as two or two and a half years since at that age he/she should be able to locate the key by its color whether or not he/she has any idea what happens when the key is pressed. With a slightly older child, or after using the color of the key for some time, you can interchange it with the actual name of the key and say "press the clear key, the red one at the top of the calculator." Finally, you will be able to refer to the key by its name without any reference to the color although the child will most likely still use the color to locate it. With a child of three or older you can even add on the purpose to be served by pressing the clear key. A good way to do this is as if the calculator were a game, such as talking about the numbers on the screen and instructing the child to "make the numbers go away by pressing the red key." After a while the key phrase "make the numbers on the display go away" will automatically indicate to the child to press the clear key and they will enjoy the power this ability to make numbers go away or disappear gives them.

Activity #3: Recognition of Error Messages

While a pre-schooler cannot be expected to understand what an error message really is or what it signifies, they can learn to recognize error messages as a "different type" of display from the ordinary numbers they usually see. This is important since there is great variety in the ways different calculators indicate an illegal operation (as we saw in Chapter 4), and it is difficult for the child or even for some adults to be able to recognize the difference between an ordinary and acceptable display and a display that fits into the category of an error message. Once the child is able to recognize the difference between these two types of display, even if he/she has no idea what the difference means or signifies, it will be easier later on when illegal operations are encountered for him/her to understand the common purpose all these different types of error message serve and to recognize and accept new error message types if they are encountered.

Since error messages differ from ordinary calculator displays in that they generally consist of letters ("E"), or words ("Error"), or strange numbers or movements (the "0.0.0.0.0.0.0.0." on my Sharp Elsi-Mate or the numbers continuously blinking on and off on my Texas Instruments TI-57), I have found it easy and clearcut to refer to this category of display as "letters" or "funny numbers." My three-year-old son Timothy likes this terminology and seems to have no trouble whatsoever in recognizing when a display fits this category of letters or funny numbers and when it doesn't. Because of this there is no question he will find it quite easy to recognize error messages when he comes across them in school use of calculators, both the error messages he is now familiar with and new ones he encounters that he has not seen before. In fact, a game I like to play with Timothy is to ask him to turn on a particular calculator and "get" either a word or a funny number in display, depending on which calculator he happens to be playing with at the time. He has become quite good at remembering the keys that I show him to press to obtain these displays, and at finding new key combinations of his own. For example, he knows that turning the calculator on or clearing the display and then pressing a key with "log" or "ln" on it will give him what he wants although he has no idea why (the logarithm of zero is undefined so pressing log or ln when zero is in the display is an illegal operation). He is very delighted with himself whenever he can get an error message in display and loves to show off this achievement whenever we have friends or relatives visiting. Try this "funny number" game with your child on several different calculators periodically, and alternate showing him/her how to get such numbers until he/she can repeat the keys himself/herself and letting him/her try to simply play with the keys in an attempt to get a funny number to appear. He/she will not only enjoy the game, he/she will also be learning something about the calculator that will be of great use later on.

Activity #4: Use of the Memory Key

The memory key on a calculator is one of the most useful extra keys there is, but most people whose calculators have this key never make the slightest use of it. This might be because they don't quite know how to use it and are afraid that if they try to they will make some mistake and ruin the problem they are working on. By encouraging the pre-schooler to use the memory key and understand what it does, you provide him/her with the knowledge and practice that will enable him/her to make use of it in numerical calculations to simplify and shorten calculator computation when such situations occur in later mathematics.

The best way to help your child learn about the memory key is by talking to him/her about making the calculator "remember" something. For example, if he/she has entered a string of eight 2s into the calculator's display, you might ask if he/she would like to see you make the calculator remember these numbers. You can then press the appropriate memory key and even when your child "makes the numbers disappear" by pressing the clear key the simple pressing of the memory recall key will show that the calculator has indeed remembered the child's numbers. Pretty soon the child will want to know how to make the calculator remember numbers himself/herself, and you can show him/her and help him/her practice until it is learned. You can also play guessing games using the calculator's memory. For example, you can put a one digit number in memory and then clear the display. Then your child can try to guess the number with you providing periodic clues like "it's bigger than five" or "it's between one and four." When he/she finally guesses the correct number and you tell him/her so, he/she can press the memory recall key to bring the hidden number back into display and verify that he/she really did get the number right. Then he/she can "hide " a number and you can do the guessing. If you have a musical calculator with a memory, you can even play a tune by pressing the appropriate keys (like *Happy Birthday* or *Twinkle, Twinkle Little Star*), and then have the calculator "remember" both the numbers entered and the corresponding song in its memory to be played back as often as you like by pressing the memory recall key. You can even alert the child to the display message or symbol (often an "M" for "Memory") that usually appears whenever a value is being remembered in memory and how that symbol can be made to disappear together with the value in memory by pressing the memory clear key. Learning to use special keys like the memory keys on a calculator is like learning to swim or learning to speak a foreign language. If you learn it when you are young it is generally easier than trying to learn it when you are older, and it will be available to you later on when you really need and want it. Play the "remember" and "guessing" games on the calculator with your child and it will serve him/her well for years to come.

Activity #5: Practice with the "Plus-Minus" or "Change Sign" Key

As we explained earlier in Chapter 4, calculators need, and usually have, a special key for giving a value a negative sign so that arithmetic with negative numbers can be carried out on the calculator. This early playtime is a good opportunity to make the child aware of this key so that he/she will know it exists and what symbol to look for on the keyboard to locate it.

At some point when you and your child are playing with the calculator and entering numbers into the display and making them either change or go away, suggest pressing the "plus-minus" or "change sign" key and looking at the display to see what it does. At first the child may not notice anything since all that is happening is that a negative sign is appearing to the left of the digits in display. In fact, on some calculators the negative sign appears way over on the left of the screen rather than just to the left of the digits and this is even less likely to be observed since the child's attention will be on the digits. Just tell the child to keep looking at the display as you keep pressing the key. What should catch his/her eye is the alternate appearance and disappearance of the negative sign. When he/she does notice that something is happening ask what it is and see that the child realizes that pressing this key makes a "dash" or "line" or "negative sign" appear and disappear from the left of the display. You can now, periodically when the calculator is being played with, suggest that the dash be made to appear until the child remembers the key this is done with and how pressing the key will make the dash appear and disappear alternately. Older students sometimes find it hard to remember that the negative sign key must be pressed *after* the number it is to go with has been entered because when we say the name of a negative number we say the sign before we say the numerical value ("negative four," not "four negative") and so they tend to try to press the keys in the order corresponding to how they say it. By having the preschooler think of the dash as separate from the number in display, and the game as "giving the number in display a dash or a negative sign," they are learning the correct way of thinking of using the plus-minus or change sign key when negative numbers are to be entered into the calculator's display.

Activity #6: Automatic Shut-Off or Power-Off

As mentioned in Chapter 4, some calculators have this special feature which automatically shuts the power off, or just clears the display, if the calculator has been left on for a certain amount of time with no key being pressed.

If one of your calculators has this feature, find out ahead of time how long the calculator must be left before this feature goes into action. If it is only a minute or so then you can tell your child during calculator playtime one day that you can magically make the numbers showing in the display disappear. Make sure there is some non-zero value in display at the time so that while you are saying all of this to your child some of that necessary one minute or so of waiting time is passing; otherwise waiting a full minute or two just watching may be too much for your child to endure in silence and inaction. As your child watches, and the required time passes, the digits in display will disappear, apparently by themselves. You can now either turn the calculator back on if it really has turned itself off, or recall the digits back into display by pressing the equal key if the calculator allows this. Then show your child how this is done by just letting time pass and ask him/her if he/she would like to do this trick for his/her other parent or anyone else who happens to be around. Go with him/her and have him/her enter several digits and then explain that the numbers will automatically and magically disappear if they just keep watching. This explanation should be made a part of the trick since it uses up some of the waiting time necessary for the feature to work. Then, if the equal key can bring the value back into the display, you can suggest that your child "bring the numbers back by pressing the equal key," pointing it out to him/her and letting him/her do the actual pressing of the key.

Keep in mind when thinking about trying, or actually trying, this activity that a pre-schooler's attention span and ability to remain quiet and inactive are very limited. If the calculator takes three or four minutes to power-off or shut-off then this is probably too long for a pre-schooler to wait. Even one minute can be too long to just sit and watch so talking about what is going to happen and then how to get the machine back on or bring the numbers back into display is necessary to keep the child's attention and pass the time. Just remember to remind the child to look at the display screen before the time is all passed since seeing the numbers actually disappear is the most enjoyable and fascinating part of the trick for the child.

Activity #7: Looking at the Display To Verify What You Enter

One of the unavoidable hazards of using a calculator is that we sometimes press the wrong key by accident, or press two keys when we really want one because they are so close together, or get two repetitions of the key we press because the calculator keyboard is excessively sensitive to the touch. In order to be sure we get what we want to get on the calculator it is necessary to develop the habit of looking at the display after pressing the digits we want in order to verify that what has appeared is what we want to appear. This does seem contrary to what typists are taught; that is, to type without looking at the typewriter keyboard or the paper, only at what is being typed from, to increase speed. But the typist has the finished paper to look at later for verification and correction; on the calculator all we get is the answer unless we are using a printing calculator. For the calculator user the most important quality is correct entry with speed a desired, but secondary, consideration.

Helping your child learn to look at the display and verify the entry is really very easy. Simply ask your child to "put" certain digits or digit combinations into the display, such as "2," or "22," or "1 2 3 4 5." Each time, follow up by saying something like "let's see if you got it" and looking at the display with him/her. If it is correct, say so to reinforce this splendid accomplishment and do another one. To your child the best reward is your approval so don't be stingy with approval. Even if the display is not correct, you can still say something like "that's not exactly right but it's very close. Let's try it again." Don't ever be negative since that takes all the enjoyment away from the game. Be positive and gently remind the child each time to "look to see if it's right." This is the habit you want to cultivate.

ACTIVITIES FOR MATHEMATICS PRE-LEARNING

Activity #8: Counting in Order from 1 to 10

Counting in order from 1 to 10 is an extremely important skill that is made use of in Kindergarten and first grade in several ways. One of the most basic uses of this skill is in counting the number of objects in a group. This is usually accomplished by young children by touching or pointing to the objects one at a time and counting as the objects are touched. If, for example, there are six objects, the child would be encouraged to touch them one at a time and count "one, two, three, four, five, six. There are six of them." The child who comes into this situation already able to count automatically from 1 to 10 can proceed more easily to counting numbers of objects than the child who must first learn to count from 1 to 10 or who has not yet mastered this skill.

A second learning experience that builds on being able to count in order from 1 to 10 is the precursor to simple arithmetic mentioned at the beginning of this chapter. When the teacher asks "What comes after five?" the child does it at first by counting from 1 to 5 and then seeing what comes next. This can then evolve into the more mathematical question "What is 5 plus 1 more?" which is really simple arithmetic. Eventually the child can be shown two piles of similar objects, like a group of four apples and a group of three apples, and asked how many there are all together when the four and the three are combined or added together. The child in the early grades does this by counting the first group "one, two, three, four" and then continuing from that point with the apples from the second group "five, six, seven" to discover that four and three all together add up to seven.

To help your child acquire this counting skill just encourage him/her to press the digit keys as they are arranged on the keyboard from 1 to 9 (since 10 is a two digit number there is no one key on the calculator that gives it so simply leave it out) and say along with you the numbers as they are pressed. Then look with him/her at the display to see the nice pattern and recite the numbers in order again. You can vary this a bit by not always going all the way up to nine. That is, sometimes press and count 1 to 5, sometimes 1 to 7, with 1 to 9 thrown in frequently for completeness. Try not to start from numbers other than 1 such as 2 to 9 or 4 to 9 until the child has mastered counting from 1 to any other one digit number since the child who learns only to count from 2 on up may count objects by starting with 2 instead of 1. Habits are hard to break so make sure the child develops the correct habit before varying from it.

Activity #9: Counting Forward from a Value Other than 1

As mentioned above, the first grader or Kindergartner will generally add two numbers together, like 4 and 3, by counting from 1 up to 4 and counting three more after that to get the result. Eventually, he/she should progress to being able to start with the first number directly and simply progress from there as in "four and three more makes five, six, seven." This requires being able to count forward, in order, from values other than 1 as the starting point.

To help with this on the calculator, make sure first that the child can easily and automatically count forward from 1, and then simply add a little variety by saying "now how about counting from 2 to 9"; then "3 to 9"; etc. Eventually, he/she should be able to count forward from any particular starting point, although in counting how many objects there are in one group he/she should always be reminded the first object is counted as "1."

Activity #10: Counting Backward in Order

Counting backward easily and fairly automatically is used to learn about "taking away" or "subtraction." The first hint of this is when the question "What comes after five?" changes to "What comes before five?" At first the child will most likely try to do this by counting "up to" five and trying to see or remember what came just before reaching five, a not inconsiderable task given the limitations on a child's memory and abstract thinking ability. Eventually it is desirable for the child to be able to think of the given number five as part of the sequence "four, five, six" so that the "after" and "before" questions can be answered without getting to five through one up to four. At a later time the child will be introduced to questions like "If there are five apples on a table and John takes three of them away how many are left on the table?" with accompanying pictures for illustration. The child is then encouraged to answer such a question by starting with the given number of apples and counting backwards to get "five apples, then take away three apples to get five, four, three, two so there will be two apples left." When the child is later introduced to the visual "number line" for the generalization of arithmetic from non-negative numbers only, to negative numbers as well, this approach to adding and subtracting by counting forward or backward from a given starting point will be used to extend addition and subtraction to negative numbers. For example, to perform the subtraction $5 - 8$ the child will be told to "start" at the number 5 and go backward or to the left 8 units" (see Figure 7.1). Doing this the child will come to rest at the final position -3 by moving the finger backwards from 5 and saying "five, four, three, two, one, zero, negative one, negative two, negative three. The answer is negative three."

$$5 - 8 = -3$$

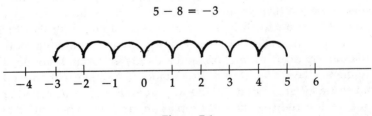

Figure 7.1

To help your child in acquiring this ability to count backward just use the same procedures outlined in activities #8 and #9. After the child has pretty well mastered counting forward from different starting values, ask him/her to count backward and count the numbers with him/her as a guide until he/she can do it by himself/herself. Begin by counting backward from nine and then try other starting points after this begins to become automatic. Don't push any of this since it is to some extent going counter to the counting forward he/she has just previously been trying to learn. Besides, you have months and even a year or two for him/her to become skilled at it before it will actually be needed in Kindergarten, first, or second grade.

Activity #11: Becoming Familiar with the Special Shapes of the Different Numerals

One of the skills elementary school children often have trouble with is writing, or "drawing," the numerals from 0 through 9. While recognizing the difference between numerals and pairing the shape with the name is itself a skill that takes time to develop, being able to draw the numerals is much more difficult than simply recognizing them. One reason for this is the difficulty children have in fine motor movements and the coordination it takes to hold a pen or pencil or crayon halfway or more up its length and still be able to guide it to make the desired results on the paper at the bottom of it. Just consider how difficult it is for an inexperienced adult to try and manipulate a pair of chopsticks in a Chinese restaurant, given all the practice the adult has had in fine motor movement and coordination through years of writing, drawing, and painting, and you'll have some idea of how difficult it is for a child to learn to draw numerals. Another reason for this difficulty is the variety of strokes the drawing of numerals requires. While a 1 requires nothing more than an up or down motion, and a 0 only an around motion, a numeral like 5 requires an across motion, a down motion, and an around (but not quite all the way around) motion all together and in the right sequence, proportion, and arrangement. The practice the pre-schooler gets in drawing numerals will pay off not only in the mathematics classroom but in the English and penmanship classroom as well since the strokes used to draw numerals are the same strokes that are used to draw legible and correct letters.

The first thing you should do to prepare the pre-schooler for learning to draw numerals is to make certain that any calculator he/she has access to and makes use of has a clear display and shows a good representation of the numerals 0 through 9. If the calculator displays a hard to recognize or even somewhat incorrect version of a numeral, this may not cause you any inconvenience in using the calculator and recognizing the answers that appear in display but it will not help and might even hurt the progress of the child in first learning to recognize the correct form of the numerals and then being able to repeat them by hand. So make sure the numerals in display, and in fact the numerals as they appear on the keys themselves, are clear and correct.

Now, have the child press individual numeral keys, but before he/she does take his/her finger in your hand and trace out, near the key, the shape of the numeral and say out loud what the shape is as you trace it out. For example, you might say "Let's press the 7 key a lot of times and see all the 7s appear on the display. Here's the 7 key. See, the 7 starts up high at the left, then we go across to the right and down across to the bottom on the left side." Then let the child press the 7 key over and over to fill the display with 7s and, as you and he/she look at the display to verify that it is in fact filled with those 7s you wanted, repeat that all the 7s start up high at the left, go across to the right and then down across to the bottom on the left side again.

There is one calculator that is especially helpful for this extremely important early learning activity, although it certainly was not designed specifically for this purpose and you can still do the activity without it on any ordinary calculator with clear and correct display. This is a gadgety type of calculator on which the keys for each digit are not really keys at all but actually enlarged versions of those digits. In other words, the key for 0 is an enlarged numeral 0, the key for 1 is an enlarged numeral 1, and so on; and they are in a variety of bright colors. This is a perfectly good and useful calculator for ordinary arithmetic purposes, so if you buy it for use in this activity it can also be used for your own needs and with your child for the other activities given here as well. With this calculator the child can actually trace out the shape of the numeral on the key, and feel its vertical and horizontal and curved parts, before pressing it to make the corresponding numerals appear on the display. This is much better than tracing out the shape by just looking at the numeral on a regular calculator key since the motions made by the child in following the contours of these numeral keys is exactly what the child will be doing with a pencil or crayon in his/her hand when he/she is learning to draw the numerals. If you cannot or do not want to get this special calculator, you can still do this activity and it is important enough that you certainly should do it; but if you can get the calculator it will make the activity much more effective and fun. So look around in special mail order catalogs or in good department stores for this numeral key calculator.

Activity #12: Adding a One-Digit Number to Itself

In elementary school one of the topics taught in the first grade is the addition of a one-digit number with itself such as 1 + 1 = 2, 2 + 2 = 4, and so on. Not only does this teach the student these particular elementary additions, it also paves the way for others that can be solved by thinking of them as modifications of these. For example, once the student knows that 5 + 5 = 10, he/she can be guided to find 5 + 6 by thinking "6 is 1 more than 5 so 5 + 6 should be 1 more than 5 + 5 or 10. So 5 + 6 is 11." Similarly, the student is guided to find 5 + 4 by thinking "4 is 1 less than 5 so 5 + 4 should be 1 less than 5 + 5 or 10. So 5 + 4 is 9." Here's a way of giving your pre-schooler a look ahead at this skill and practice in becoming familiar with adding a one-digit number to itself.

For this activity you simply make use of the fact that adding a value to itself is equivalent to multiplying it by two, and the constant key that many calculators have. Simply set up the calculator with such a constant key for multiplication by 2 so that all you have to do is enter a new number into display, press the equal key, and twice the number you entered will appear in the display as a result. If you don't recall how this is done go back to Chapter 4 where the use of the constant key is described. You can now enter any one-digit value into display, ask your child if he/she can tell you what the result is when that value is added to itself, and then let him/her press the equal key to get the correct answer in display and see if he/she was right. For variety he/she can also enter a value and you can "guess" its double and verify by pressing the equal key.

Activity #13: Summing to Ten

Another skill that students are taught in early elementary school is that of finding what must be added to a one-digit number to give a total of 10. This skill is then used to extend addition of two one-digit numbers that have a one-digit sum to addition of two one-digit numbers that have a two-digit sum. For example, suppose the student is given the addition problem $7 + 5$. The child who has already learned that when 3 is added to 7 the result is 10 is taught to reason out $7 + 5$ by saying or thinking "Let's see. Seven and 3 more make 10, so if we take away 3 of the 5 to go with the 7 we get 10 and 2 left over from the 5 makes 12." This is just the solution $7 + 5 = 7 + 3 + 2 = 10 + 2 = 12$ on a much less mathematical and more intuitive level. To give your pre-schooler exposure to the process of summing to 10, and some practice in actually using it, use the following calculator activity.

Enter any one-digit number into the display and ask the child how much more is needed to get a total of 10. The child can get an answer in a variety of ways, including counting up from the displayed value to 10, one at a time; or holding up as many fingers as are needed to represent the displayed digit and then counting from 1 up as the remaining "down" fingers are raised until all 10 fingers are raised; or by taking a set of 10 objects like counters or apples or colored blocks that you have supplied for him/her, taking away the number corresponding to the displayed digit and counting the number remaining from the original 10. However the answer is obtained, you can then use the calculator to add this answer to the number already in display and see if the sum is in fact 10. When you press the addition key to obtain the sum use a word like "and" (3 "and" 7 gives) so the child gets the feeling of the two numbers being somehow combined and the addition key doing the combining. If the result that appears in display is 10 then the child's answer was correct and you should tell him/her so and congratulate him/her. If not, then say so but also give encouragement and approval anyway for a good try and then do it correctly with him/her, showing how you get the answer in a way he/she can understand. Eventually, the child will begin automatically to pair the correct values together like 1 and 9, 2 and 8, 3 and 7, and so on. This automatic pairing without having to work out the correct second number of the pair is exactly what will later enable the child, when he/she reaches elementary school, correctly and efficiently to advance to addition of two one-digit numbers that sum to a two-digit number.

Activity #14: Counting Forward by Values Other than 1, such as by 2s or 3s

After your child has been in elementary school for a few years, he/she will encounter simple multiplication of two one-digit numbers. The usual way such simple multiplication is first introduced is as repeated addition, as in the statement "4 times 2 is the same as adding 2 to itself 4 times. So 4 times 2 is 2, 4, 6, 8 or 8." Since adding a number to itself several times can be thought of as counting forward by that amount at a time, exposure to such counting can help ready a child for that first encounter with multiplication when it occurs in the elementary classroom.

To employ this activity it is necessary to first determine whether or not your calculator has the capability of counting forward by any desired amount at a time. Since this feature is a by-product of how a calculator operates, and is not a feature that a manufacturer specifically builds into a calculator or is even aware of, the only way to determine whether a particular machine has it is to actually try it out. To do this, try out the following two keystroke sequences on your calculator:

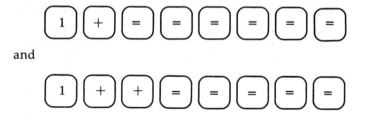

and

If either of these two keystroke sequences causes your display to show the values 1, 2, 3, 4, etc. in order, then the calculator does have this counting capability. If neither works, then simply do not use this activity or look for a calculator that does count and buy it for use in this activity.

If your calculator was able to "count" by ones, then you can make it count by twos (2, 4, 6, 8, . . .) or threes (3, 6, 9, 12, . . .) or any other amount by simply replacing the 1 in the keystroke sequence above that worked on your calculator with 2, 3, or whatever number you want to count by. To begin with, set up your calculator to count by ones and then, together with your child, count in order as you press the equals key over and over again and the integers appear in succession on the display. Then set it up and let your child press the equals key to make the calculator "count" with you and the child counting along together. After a while you can set up the calculator to count by twos instead of ones. This will be strange and possibly even disturbing to the child since he/she will not at first appreciate that there is in fact a pattern of alternate integers, and may simply see these as some of the integers with certain values left out. After a while, however, he/she will begin to remember this sequence by rote the same way he/she originally remembered the integers 1, 2, 3, 4, and so on when they were first encountered. If you want to, you can make a list of the integers from 1 to 20 in order and point out as the calculator "counts" by twos that the numbers that appear are just the alternate ones on the list. Finally, once counting by twos begins to be accepted and remembered you can use your list of integers from 1 to 20 to point out and circle every third number in the list and then show your child how the calculator can count by threes and get exactly this sequence of numbers. Keep in mind that you are not, repeat not, attempting to teach your pre-schooler to multiply two one-digit numbers. Unless the pre-schooler is extremely advanced and precocious, he/she simply would not be ready for something like this. What you are doing is exposing him/her to sequences of integers different from, but similar to, the sequence of all integers from 1 upward 1 at a time so that he/she will begin to feel familiar and comfortable with these patterns and have some remembrance of them when they are encountered later on in elementary school and used to help in learning simple multiplication.

Index